"For whatever reason, one of the oldest and fondest D&D memories I have burned into my mind is the recipe for Otik's Skillet-Fried Spiced Potatoes in *Leaves from the Inn of the Last Home*. It makes me so happy that Kyle, Jon, Michael, and company are carrying the torch for the next generation with this cookbook. P.S. Try the Halfling Chili . . ."

—JOE MANGANIELLO, actor, producer, author, and
   D&D collaborator

"Whether you're a human craving a belly-warming Traveler's Stew or an elf in need of Qualinesti Stew, this book is a lot of fun and the food is easy and delicious. Tons of quick, simple recipes for your local tabletop crew, your family, or both. If you cook, get this book. If you don't cook, get this book and give it to someone who will cook for you."

—FREDDIE PRINZE JR.

"All are welcome to join this world of create-your-own-adventure-style cooking, baking, and mixology to compliment even the most intense game nights. There are so many magical masterpieces and delicious delicacies—diverse enough to suit the tastes of even the hungriest and pickiest creatures. No matter what realm you reside in, the recipes will have you feeling well prepared and equipped for your own culinary quest. As a baker myself, I can't wait to try the Halfling's Rose Apple and Blackberry Pie! Yum! Everyone is a winner with this book."

—KATHERINE MCNAMARA, actor and baker

"Casting, attacking, dodging, delving . . . a hero works up an appetite. Kyle, Jon, and Michael's cookbook isn't just a novelty; this is really good stuff to add that extra dimension to your campaign. Remember, a well-fed DM is bound to take it easier on you!"

—CRAIG MAZIN, writer/producer, *Chernobyl*

DUNGEONS & DRAGONS®

HEROES' FEAST

The Official Dungeons & Dragons Cookbook

KYLE NEWMAN • JON PETERSON • MICHAEL WITWER

RECIPES BY ADAM RIED

PHOTOGRAPHS BY RAY KATCHATORIAN

TEN SPEED PRESS
California | New York

CONTENTS

1

HUMAN CUISINE · 1

2

ELVEN CUISINE · 51

3

DWARVEN CUISINE · 83

4

HALFLING CUISINE · 113

5

UNCOMMON CUISINE · 147

6

ELIXIRS & ALES · 179

INTRODUCTION

What is Dungeons & Dragons? For some, it's a dynamic narrative game with infinite possibilities; for others, an exciting tactical contest of strategy and wit. But for many, it is far more than a game; it's a way of life.

If you're holding this book, then you probably love two things: D&D and sharing a great meal. And why shouldn't you? Few things go together so well: they're tabletop activities and highly social occasions, and both offer endless possibilities. But the similarities run far deeper. No matter where you are in the world, food is at the center of community and connection. For millions of fans, D&D plays very much the same role. You might say that D&D is the food of the imagination.

Dungeons & Dragons is no ordinary game, and this is no ordinary cookbook; it's a uniquely D&D cookbook. Inside, you'll find familiar recipes and dishes that were only available to your D&D player characters, until now—an adventure of food! We began this quest with a simple inquiry: how can food elevate and enhance the D&D experience? If the magic of D&D springs from its ability to activate the human imagination, then how can we recast that same enchantment over an inspiring set of recipes? In short, we want this book to be an essential part of your game nights. Why put out a bag of chips when you can prepare a batch of Halfling Oatmeal Sweet Nibbles (page 128)? Or perhaps you're craving the same Iron Rations (page 8) as your dungeon-delving character to sustain you through the game. Which protein will flavor your Sword Coast Seafood Bouillabaisse (page 11)? Maybe you should roll for it. If you are new to the kitchen, try a lower-level recipe to start! Our goal is to stimulate the spirit of adventure at your gaming table and beyond by inviting you to enter a new culinary dimension.

Here you will find a curated selection of D&D recipes spanning the vast multiverse. They are all delicious, easy to prepare, and composed of ingredients readily found in this realm. Even better, these recipes offer a unique opportunity to enhance the social experience that is D&D, whether it happens to be a game night or you just wish it were. Because D&D is bound only by the limits of the imagination, without an agreed-upon singular storyline or locale, we have organized this cookbook by one of the game's few ubiquitous devices: the multitude of playable fantasy groups featured in D&D's 5th edition. This structure invites D&D and fantasy lovers alike to eat like their favorite fictional cultures—from elves and dwarves to orcs and drow—while we shed fresh light on their stories via their unique cuisines and lifestyles.

Dungeons & Dragons is about far more than monsters or treasure; it's built on the foundation of community, friendship, and imagination. This culinary compendium will inspire and encourage those same principles through the art and craft of cooking, while adding an exciting and visceral new layer to your game nights: sights, smells, touch, and, of course, *tastes*.

So, what is Dungeons & Dragons? Join us as we find our answer through the dishes and cuisine that make this multiverse so delicious.

About This Book: Creating Food and Water

The culinary canvas of the D&D multiverse is no different than the game itself: it's bound only by the imagination. However, Dungeons & Dragons is also rich with real-world influences, drawing heavily from our own past as well as fictional realms created by some of the world's greatest dreamers. Roast meats, hearty grains, cooked vegetables, and other familiar staples dominate the in-world menus from the castles of Krynn to the taverns of the Forgotten Realms of Toril. And while the worlds of D&D have many similarities to our own, unless you have a kitchen full of magical items, knowledge of powerful spells, and access to an array of mystical ingredients, you won't be able to prepare many of its recipes in their original forms. And let's be honest, many foods referenced in D&D materials are not quite right for the modern Earth palate (crisped worm skewers, anyone?).

Fear not, brave adventurer! We've put together dishes that are not only true to their various worlds, but also tasty and possible to prepare here in ours. Can't find rothé meat at the local butcher? Don't worry—grass-fed beef or buffalo will do. Trying to find a substitute for cockatrice? Well, it's said that everything tastes like cockatrice, so chicken should suffice. Our methodology in creating this recipe collection was simple: find every notable dish, ingredient, and recipe in the D&D multiverse; curate and modify it for feasibility, appropriateness, and, most important, flavor; and present it here in a way that even a 1st level chef might be able to make it for game night. Accordingly, our master chef has not only provided easy-to-follow recipes but also some helpful "Cook's Notes" that will guide you through every aspect of the journey. "So enjoy, and may the dice be good to you!"

Adventuring Equipment

Like a red dragon's lair, the road of culinary adventure is fraught with both peril and reward. Only with a fair amount of attention to detail, ingenuity, and luck do you have a chance of survival. But you'll also need the right equipment. Whether it be the sword for the fighter or the spellbook for the magic-user, all adventurers need the proper tools of the trade to ensure their success. Here are some implements that will help you complete this adventure and hopefully gain some experience along the way:

- **Cheese grater**
- **Cocktail shaker and muddler**
- **Dutch oven or heavy-bottomed pan**
- **Food processor**
- **Measuring cups and spoons**
- **Pastry brush**
- **Pie plate**
- **Strainer**
- **Stand mixer or electric hand-mixer**
- **Tongs**
- **Wire rack**

A Digestible Cookbook

Distilling forty-five years of D&D culinary traditions, dishes, ingredients, and flavors is a formidable task and one that requires an appropriately comprehensive approach. To this end, we have endeavored to provide as many angles and perspectives as possible to guide you through this delicious journey. Here are a few thematic devices we used to unlock this multiverse of flavor:

HEROES' FEASTS

Bad news. You've been teleported into Acererak's Chamber of Hopelessness. A magical inscription on the wall reads: "You who dared to violate my tomb now pay the price. Stay here and die slowly of starvation, or open and enter the door to the south, where certain but quick death awaits." Good news! You're locked in with an 11th level druid who can cast Heroes' Feast once per day, ensuring you certainly won't starve to death as the inscription had predicted. But . . . bad news again: your druid is particularly fond of liver and anchovies, and you can be sure the rest of your days will be spent eating nothing but gamy and briny morsels. The south door is looking better and better, or maybe you'll just starve to death after all.

All Heroes' Feasts are not the same. They are often left open to the tastes, preferences, and skills of the casters themselves, all of which can lead to significant variation. This is further compounded by the eclectic eating preferences of each fantasy culture. Would an elven cleric make the same Heroes' Feast as a half-orc druid? Not likely. While we can't account for all possible variations of this spell, we do know that it is a multicourse meal of "magnificent food and drink," which has significant restorative properties. To this end, we have defined what the Heroes' Feast might look like across the different fantasy folk, and when you see the below icons, it means that the recipe should be included in a proper Heroes' Feast for that culture.

MAGNIFICENT MENUS

All establishments in the D&D multiverse, whether humble roadside taverns or lofty banquet halls, have a time, place, and purpose, but some have undeniably stood out above the rest. In this recurring feature, we want to provide an in-world glance at the fare of some of the most renowned establishments located throughout some of D&D's most storied locales. Look for the asterisks on each menu denoting which recipes are included in the book.

HEROES' FEAST RECIPES

HUMAN

14
Amphail
Braised Beef

27
Vedbread

39
Castle Amber
Onion Soup

43
Gingerbread Man

ELVEN

59
High Harvest
Puree

63
Wood Elf
Forest Salad

75
Dragon Salmon

79
Meal's End

DWARVEN

97
Potato Leek Soup

99
Smoked Sausages
and Kraut with
Dwarven Mustard

103
Dwarven Flatbread

109
Black Pudding

HALFLING

127
Melted Cheeses with
Chunky Tomato Broth

131
Lluirwood Salad

135
Honeyed Ham
with Pineapple Gravy

139
Heartlands Rose Apple
and Blackberry Pie

Worlds of Flavor

While Dungeons & Dragons doesn't have a single, agreed-upon world or storyline, from a culinary standpoint there are a few locales that have stood out above the rest. The core campaign worlds that inspired the recipes from this book include:

Forgotten Realms

Created by Ed Greenwood, the *Forgotten Realms* is a rich, high-fantasy setting full of colorful characters and diverse locales. Rooted on an Earth-like planet called Abeir-Toril (*Toril* for short), this sprawling campaign world hosts a wide variety of features, from dense medieval-style metropolises and ports, impenetrable castles and fortresses, and one-horse hamlets to thick forests, rolling meadows, craggy mountains, and vast deserts, all spread across several key continents, including Kara-Tur, Zakhara, Maztica, and, most famously, Faerûn (and the Underdark that exists below its surface). Faerûn boasts some of the game's most storied locations, including the areas and regions of the Sword Coast, the Savage Frontier, the Dalelands, Calimshan, Chult, Cormyr, Thay, Amn, and Icewind Dale, as well as the legendary cities of Neverwinter, Waterdeep, Baldur's Gate, Calimport, and the notorious Underdark city of Menzoberranzan. The cuisine of Toril is as varied as the settings themselves, from dishes inspired by traditional medieval Europe to tastes derived from the Middle East, Asia, as well as the Americas.

Greyhawk

The brainchild of D&D co-creator Gary Gygax, *Greyhawk* is a gritty, sword-and-sorcery-style world full of deadly dungeons and forbidden, arcane magic. This campaign is set on another Earth-like planet with medieval sensibilities—a geocentric globe called Oerth. Similar to Earth, Oerth has several continents, including Hepmonaland, Hyperboria, and, most notably, Oerik, which hosts an area on its eastern part commonly referred to as the Flanaess. The Flanaess is home to Greyhawk's most famous regions and kingdoms, including Perrenland, the Shield Lands, Urnst, Luz, Veluna, Keoland, Sunndi, and Furyondy. Fabled cities and dungeons dot these areas from the Free City of Greyhawk, the Village of Hommlet, and White Plume Mountain to Saltmarsh, Blackmoor, and beyond. Greyhawk's cuisine is primarily inspired by dishes from feudal Europe, especially the tavern fare and game of medieval Britain and other areas throughout mainland Europe, sometimes with a fantastical, or even otherworldly twist.

Eberron

A creation of Keith Baker, *Eberron* is a world of swashbuckling, pulpy adventure where elaborate mechanisms and powerful magic exist side by side. The planet Eberron comprises several continents, the most famous of which is Khorvaire. There, the eclectic five nations of Aundair, Breland, the Mournland (Cyre), Karrnath, and Thrane yearn for supremacy over the ruined Kingdom of Galifar. From the towers and sky ships of Sharn to the ruin-filled port city of Stormreach, this whimsical, post-war campaign has something for everyone, including its cuisine, which boasts extraordinary variety across the five nations. The flavors of Eberron range from simple medieval-style fare to highly refined and complex gastronomic concoctions made with Victorian sensibilities using a combination of magic and machines.

Dragonlance

Developed by Tracy Hickman and Margaret Weis, *Dragonlance* is a dreamy, high-fantasy world of purple mountains, evergreen trails, crystal lakes, and dragons

of every color. Dragonlance's campaign world of Krynn is one of opposing polarities where magic is rare and natural-born enemies are tasked with working together to maintain cosmic balance and avoid total destruction. Ansalon is the most well-known of the planet's five continents, and it includes many of the famous locations from the campaign's bestselling novels, including Solace, Qué-Shu, Pax Tharkas, Tarsis, Xak Tsaroth, Istar, Qualinost, Silvanost, Solamnia, and beyond. The fare of this lush world ranges from traditional medieval tavern and peasant food to distinctive flavors from the Middle East and Asia.

Other Worlds

In addition to the previously mentioned realms, there are myriad other worlds in the Dungeons & Dragons pantheon, which are nearly as numerous as the players themselves. From the scorched plains of Athas in Dark Sun to the cruel mists of Barovia in gothic Ravenloft, all are united by the mystical gateways of Planescape. There truly is no limit to D&D or the worlds in which it lives.

Legendary Establishments

You can't go far in any D&D campaign without spending some time at a tavern, bar, inn, or eatery. These dicey locales are frequently where critical information is gathered and often where the adventure begins (or ends if you wind up getting into a deadly scuffle). Some establishments have seen more than their fair share of adventure, and the following are among D&D's most iconic.

THE YAWNING PORTAL

This iconic tavern and eatery located in the City of Waterdeep is among the most famous in the Forgotten Realms. Owned and operated by a gruff former adventurer called Durnan the Wanderer, this multilevel establishment tenders not only fine food and drink, but potential fame and fortune as well. Built atop one of D&D's largest and most notorious dungeons, the fabled Undermountain, this tavern offers paying customers entrance to the sprawling lair via a well that leads into its depths. Unfortunately, most patrons never return. For the menu, see page 48.

THE INN OF THE LAST HOME

Seated in the branches of a massive vallenwood tree, this rustic, country tavern located in the town of Solace is without a doubt the most famous establishment in the Dragonlance world. It is here where the Heroes of the Lance assemble and begin their unexpected journey among the wafting smells of fried spiced potatoes (see page 29)—a specialty of the proprietor, Otik Sandath, and often prepared by its lovely barmaid, Tika Waylan, who becomes one of the unlikely adventurers herself. Known for its strong ales, tasty food, and cozy atmosphere, the Inn of the Last Home is a can't-miss stop for those who traverse the world of Krynn. For the menu, see page 80.

CELESTIAL VISTA RESTAURANT

Floating high above Eberron's City of Sharn in the Azure District of Skyway is the city's renowned Celestial Vista Restaurant. Here, well-to-do tourists and locals alike flock for the view and the cosmopolitan cuisine—where gastronomic innovation meets the traditional dishes of the five nations. Owned by powerful city council member Evix ir'Marasha, the atmosphere is elegant, the food is purified (by House Ghallanda), and the prices are as high as the eatery itself. For the menu, see page 111.

THE GREEN DRAGON INN

Situated in the River Quarter of the Free City of Greyhawk, this iconic pub is everything you'd expect of a D&D tavern: dark, cozy, and dangerous. Hushed conversations linger over map-covered tables, while the smell of roasted game wafts heavily above the underlying stench of stale ale. Whether you're looking for tasty regional cuisine of the Flanaess or trouble, you'll find it at the Green Dragon. For the menu, see page 144.

TIPS FOR MAGICAL COOKING
Excerpt from the *Codex of Eldritch Cuisine*

The Great Library of Candlekeep, built upon the rocky cliffs of the Sword Coast, is home to the most famous and comprehensive collection of arcane texts in all of Toril. But few know that cloistered behind the library's fortressed walls resides the greatest repository of culinary knowledge as well. The exhaustive archive boasts thousands of gastronomic tomes from the greater multiverse, many scribed ages ago by long-forgotten chefs whose creations await rediscovery. The following tips were discovered in the *Codex of Eldritch Cuisine*.

Use Magic

For denizens of the multiverse, it is preferable (and much safer) to cast mage hand, and have your spectral appendage cut the vegetables for you. Of course, if you have a druid or cleric in your midst, they can simply cast heroes' feast and skip all of the fuss! If you are not so arcanely inclined, please take your time. Speed won't win you any awards in the kitchen, and severed digits will rarely improve upon any of the recipes. However, the lizardfolk recipe for Fried Fingers is an exception to this rule.

Keep Thy Blades Sharp

Chopping carrots is just like severing heads, and a dull blade simply won't get the job done. Ask any respectable half-orc chef and they will impress upon you to take the same care with a fine butcher knife as you do with a great axe.

Clean as You Cook

Staring down a sink full of sullied pots, pans, and dishes can be just as daunting as squaring off against an ancient black dragon. It's advisable to handle the cleaning duties during your downtime so that you can enjoy the meal carefree when it's ready. Unless, of course, you can cast prestidigitation to clean those dishes, then do whatever in the nine hells you please.

Plan Ahead

Manage your time and your menu to ensure the meal is ready when desired. It's advisable to read through whichever recipe before you set out to make it, to avoid surprises or missing ingredients.

Cook with Friends

If you are unable to conjure your unseen servant for sous-chef duties, then form an adventuring party for your culinary conquests. It's fun to cook with a friend or two, and okay to taste as you go.

Procure the Right Equipment

The tools of the trade must be respected. You will save much time, effort, and aggravation if you can find any of these hanging around your kitchen:

Pan of Cooking; Pan of Spicing;
Spoon of Eating; Spoon of Mixing; Spoon of Sugar;
Tablecloth of Feasting; Chalice of Liquid Food;
Book of Dinner; Apron of Comfort; Planar Fork;
Fork of Travel; Mug of Warming; Mystical Brown Coating Box;
Platter of Purity; the Eternal Salt Shaker;
Utensil of the Cultured Palate; Utensil of Etiquette.

1
HUMAN CUISINE

*"It's just as well Caramon's not here. Can you imagine
the bellyaching we'd hear about missing a couple of meals?"*

—MARGARET WEIS AND TRACY HICKMAN, *DRAGONS OF WINTER NIGHT*

No people within the multiverse are as determined and adaptable as the human race. Their thirst for knowledge, their penchant for adventure, and their indomitable spirit have rendered them a force to be reckoned with. Along with this assertive culture comes a hunger for adventure, technological advancement, and creative experimentation. It is often said that humanity is a melting pot of ideas, and the same is certainly true of its gastronomy. With such diverse people, it is difficult to define the similarities across each culture, except for perhaps this: the only constant is change; the only characteristic is variety.

A BROAD SPECTRUM

Humans of the planet Toril alone boast nine major ethnic groups, with basic physical attributes such as height and skin tone varying greatly by region. In short, there is no typical human. Seemingly undaunted by climate and topography, human civilizations have thrived in all manner of environments, and with this diversity comes an eclectic array of culinary foodways. As by far the most common people throughout the multiverse, humans and their preferences tend to set the standard at taverns and other public eating establishments when it comes to portion size, flavor, and even the very design of the tables, seating, and flatware—most of which are made to accommodate human size, human hands, and human sensibilities (sorry, halflings!). While dining etiquette, presentation, and ingredients used can vary wildly across the mélange of human cultures, one general constant seems to be the speed at which humans eat: fast. Among the most short-lived within the multiverse, humans generally seem to be in a rush while dining, no doubt eager to get back to ambitious plans of adventuring, or cultivation. This haste carries over to all aspects of their food preparation as well. Elves and dwarves, with their longer lifespans, might marinate their foods for weeks and braise their meats for days, but "slow-cooking" for humans means just a few hours, with most preparations completed in under an hour. However, this hurried nature does have its advantages; most culinary innovations, whether of physical or magical means, occur under the direction of a human, often in search of new efficiencies in preparation, or new dishes to concoct from whatever local ingredients are available.

Among the youngest of cultures in the multiverse, humans in general are far less principled or traditional about their meals. Thus, their menus abound with variety in ingredients, preparation, and presentation. For example, humans of the coasts readily dine on trout, shrimp, squid, scallops, and mussels in a medley of soups, stews, and pastas, but it's not uncommon to also find the exact same ocean-sourced proteins grilled, beer-battered, baked, spit-roasted, pan-seared, smoked, sautéed, flambéed, or even served raw. Similarly, these meals can just as easily show up on the finest porcelain and silver platters of castles and palaces as they do on the tin and wooden dishware of taverns located throughout the various worlds.

VARIETY IS THE SPICE OF LIFE

Most current human civilizations evolved out of ancestral nomadic cultures, and even today, humans are among the most well-traveled, capable of finding purchase in all types of environments. Accordingly, humans are just as likely to be hunters or adventurers as they would be farmers or foragers, and they do not tend to be fickle eaters. Animal-based protein is traditionally the desired focus of main courses, with beef, pork, lamb, fish, or chicken comprising the list of staples. However, meat is costly to procure or raise, so grains, vegetables, and fruits make up the bulk of most human meals. Human palates are far more a function of local availability than of any innate predisposition toward tastes. Humans bring their bravado to food, with adventure frequently taking precedent over tradition and function. In metropolises such as Waterdeep or Greyhawk, affluent urban dwellers might even sample monster meats such as baked stirges, roast manticore, or wyvern steaks purely for boasting rights. All flavors find their favor when the human palate is concerned. So, do humans prefer spicy or sweet; sour or salty; bitter or briny? The answer: Yes.

INGREDIENTS OF AMBITION

Barring magical means, food preservation is rudimentary and a common challenge for most of these transient people. Members of the higher classes have better means to keep ingredients fresh and thus more varied options for food preparation. Salted and dried meats, soups, stews, broths, and rations are stalwarts for the majority of human society. Most meals revolve around a protein, complemented with a starch of some sort, the usual being bread (wheat or rye) or rice, which is then paired with a local vegetable. Commoners will usually imbibe a form of beer, ale, or port, while the gentry generally favor whiskey or wine. Clean water is often a luxury, so alcohol serves as a safer beverage that also travels well.

Larger human-constructed cities are typically melting pots of cultures. Fragrant spices and far-off ingredients commonly populate bustling marketplaces, commanding premium prices. As a result, the human cupboard becomes that of the multiverse itself. With its strong agrarian roots, harvest is widely celebrated among human communities, with seasonal components providing a welcome source of change for these omnivores. Consequently, holidays such as Trolltide or Liars' Night on the famed Sword Coast or Yule Welcoming on Krynn are less religious in nature, serving to anchor the changing seasons and inform their respective menus.

Whether coastal or inland, on the trail or in the tavern, the recipes that follow are but a small sample of the diverse dishes, ingredients, and flavors that commonly show up on the human table.

Traveler's Stew

Nothing is more welcoming to the battered, trail-weary adventurer than the unmistakable scent of beef and ale wafting from a bubbling, flame-licked cauldron. Find a seat near the inn's blackened hearth and take a load off—warmth and safety are finally at hand. This earthy, slow-cooked concoction consisting of beef (or rothé), carrots, potatoes, and onions in a dark beer–infused broth is served in eating establishments everywhere, from the Green Dragon Inn and the Yawning Portal to Ellfate's Eatery and the Inn of the Last Home. Be warned traveler, it won't taste right without a wooden bowl and spoon.

In a large bowl, combine the flour, 1 teaspoon salt, and several grinds of pepper. Add the beef and toss to coat well.

Warm the oil in a large, heavy pot over medium-high heat. Add one-third to half of the beef—do not crowd—and cook for about 5 minutes, turning to brown all sides evenly. Transfer the browned beef to a plate and repeat to brown the remaining beef, adding more oil, if needed, between batches.

Pour the beer into the pot and use a wooden spoon to scrape up any browned bits. Return the browned beef to the pot and add the broth and paprika. Adjust the heat to low, cover, and cook at a simmer until the meat is very tender, 1½ to 2 hours.

Add the onion, carrots, and potatoes to the pot, and continue to simmer until the vegetables are tender, about 30 minutes. Stir in the parsley and season with salt and pepper. Serve hot.

SERVES 6

¼ cup all-purpose flour

Kosher salt and freshly ground black pepper

1½ pounds beef stew meat, cut into 1-inch pieces

1 tablespoon vegetable oil, plus more as needed

1 cup dark beer

4 cups low-sodium beef broth

1 teaspoon sweet paprika

1 large yellow onion, chopped

2 carrots, peeled and cut into ½-inch rounds

3 Yukon gold potatoes, peeled and cut into 1-inch pieces

¼ cup chopped fresh parsley

◆ COOK'S NOTE ◆

Most stews are made with broth and a small amount of wine, but this one utilizes dark beer. The beer infuses the stew with an earthy and faintly malty flavor.

Iron Rations

You won't last long anywhere in the multiverse without a few basic things: a trusty sword, a full waterskin, and some iron rations. Sometimes referred to as "journeyfood," this staple provides essential nourishment for adventurers of all sorts, from the trail-tested travelers of Ansalon to the dungeon-delving explorers of the Flanaess. While ingredients frequently vary depending on region, these rations tend to be lightweight, protein-packed, and preserved to last days or even weeks on the road, featuring ingredients such as cured meats, dried fruits, nuts, and cheeses with biscuits, crackers, or hardtack. Godspeed and good eating fair adventurer.

SERVES 4

1¼ pounds semifirm or firm cheese, such as Manchego, Asiago Fresco, Gruyère, Comté, Jarlsberg, Gouda, Monterey Jack, or Cheddar, cut into bite-size cubes

10 ounces hard salami; cured sausage, such as hard chorizo, Calabrese, pepperoni, or sopressata; or beef or turkey jerky cut into bite-size pieces

12 pitted dates, dried figs, or dried apricots

1 cup roasted nuts, such as almonds, pecans, cashews, pistachios, or a mixture

4 handfuls wheat crackers

4 whole pieces fresh fruit, such as apples, pears, bananas, oranges, or 4 small bunches grapes

If dining in, divide the cheese, salami, dried fruit, nuts, crackers, and fresh fruit among four plates, and serve. Alternatively, if you're eating on the trail, combine all the ingredients in a large container or bag (or divide evenly among four individual containers) to take with you.

◈ COOK'S NOTE ◈

If combining in a container or bag, use dried beef or turkey jerky instead of salami to prevent the mix from becoming too moist due to the high fat content of the meat.

Sword Coast Seafood Bouillaisse

You don't need to frequent Faerûnian ports such as Neverwinter, Waterdeep, or Baldur's Gate to enjoy this stewed ocean-meat medley. Served in taverns, in homesteads, and on seafaring vessels across countless realms, this eternally popular nautical dish consists of cod, or haddock, clams, and mussels simmered in a light fish and tomato stock with a licorice-flavored aperitif and a pinch of fennel. Some taverns even make theirs with an impressive serving of aldani—if they can manage to defeat one! A *rouille*—a nippy red pepper, garlic, and olive oil blend—helps complete the aromatic dish served year-round. The flavorful broth is also perfect for soaking toasted herb breads. Swashbucklers and sea rogues alike never turn down a ladleful.

In a large Dutch oven over medium heat, warm the oil until shimmering. Add the onion, bay leaves, and 1 teaspoon salt and cook, stirring, until softened, about 4 minutes. Add the leek, chopped garlic, fennel seed, red pepper flakes, and saffron (if using) and cook, stirring, until fragrant, about 1 minute more. Add the tomato paste and cook, stirring, for about 1 minute more. Add the wine, adjust the heat to medium-high, and bring to a simmer. Simmer, stirring and scraping the bottom of the pot, for about 1 minute more. Add the fish stock, tomatoes, and orange zest and return to a simmer. Adjust the heat to medium-low and simmer to blend flavors, about 20 minutes more. Pick out and discard the bay leaves and orange zest strips, if desired. Add the anise liqueur and stir to combine.

Add the clams to the pot, adjust the heat to medium-high, and bring to a simmer. Adjust the heat to medium, cover, and cook, stirring occasionally, for 5 minutes. Sprinkle the fish with salt and pepper and submerge it in the liquid in the pot, arranging it in as much of a single layer as possible around the clams. Add the mussels, replace the cover, and cook until the clams and mussels open (when serving, discard any that don't) and the fish is fully opaque and firm when gently squeezed (cooking time will depend on the type and thickness of the fish), 8 to 14 minutes more. Set aside off the heat to rest for 5 minutes.

Meanwhile, cut the remaining clove of garlic in half and swipe over the toasts, then drizzle with olive oil.

CONTINUED ON PAGE 12 →

SERVES 4 TO 6

2 tablespoons extra-virgin olive oil, plus more for drizzling

1 large yellow onion, chopped

2 bay leaves

Kosher salt

1 large leek, white and light green parts, halved lengthwise and cut into 1-inch pieces

5 garlic cloves; 4 finely chopped, 1 left whole

1½ teaspoons ground fennel seed

½ teaspoon red pepper flakes, or more if needed

¼ teaspoon crushed saffron threads (optional)

1 tablespoon tomato paste

½ cup dry white wine

2 cups fish or seafood stock

1 (14.5-ounce) can diced tomatoes

4 strips orange zest, about 4 inches long by 1 inch wide

2 tablespoons anise-flavored liqueur, such as pastis or Pernod

INGREDIENTS CONTINUED →

Sword Coast Seafood Bouillabaisse,
CONTINUED

1½ pounds littleneck clams, rinsed and scrubbed well, any gaping clams discarded

1½ pounds firm, meaty white fish fillets (such as monkfish, swordfish, hake, haddock, cod, halibut, or tilapia), skinned, if necessary, and cut into 1½-inch chunks

Freshly ground black pepper

1½ pounds mussels, debearded if necessary, rinsed and scrubbed, any gaping mussels discarded

Thick slices of baguette, pain au levain, or hearty French or Italian bread, toasted, for serving

¼ cup chopped fresh parsley

Add most of the parsley to the stew and stir gently to incorporate but try not to break up the fish too much. Taste and adjust the seasoning with salt and pepper, if necessary. Serve at once, with the toasts, in warmed shallow soup plates, drizzling each serving with some olive oil and sprinkling with the remaining parsley.

◆ COOK'S NOTE ◆

You can substitute some shelled, deveined extra-large shrimp (21 to 25 shrimp per pound) or sea scallops for a portion of the fish, keeping in mind that they will probably cook faster than some of the meatier types of fish.

Pan-Fried Knucklehead Trout

There isn't much to see and even less to eat in the frozen tundra that is Icewind Dale . . . unless you know where to look. North of the Spine of the World and hidden in the windswept shadow of Kelvin's Cairn, stand three freshwater lakes that support the ten villages that dot their shores—a region aptly known as Ten Towns. The lakes of Ten Towns are unremarkable, except for one feature: they are the only known location of the storied knucklehead trout. Named for their thick, knuckle-shaped skulls, these fish have become the region's most lucrative export, not for their culinary value but rather for the finely crafted scrimshaw that local artisans make with the ivory-like headbones. Merchants from Luskan and beyond pay top dollar for these curios, which have become all the rage throughout the cities of Faerûn. As a result, lakes of Ten Towns often run red with the blood of local fisherman competing for the day's catch. However, what's less known outside of the region is that these rare fish are as delicious as they are valuable, especially when pan-fried with shallots, lemon, salt, pepper, and paprika. If you can't source fresh knucklehead trout from the lakes of Ten Towns, don't dismay. Trout from Nyr Dyv near the City of Greyhawk or Crystalmir Lake close to Solace will suffice as substitutes.

Preheat the oven to 250°F with a rack in the middle of the oven.

In a wide, shallow dish such as a pie plate, whisk together the flour, paprika, ½ teaspoon salt, and ½ teaspoon pepper.

Sprinkle the trout fillets lightly with salt and pepper and let rest until they appear moist and glistening, about 5 minutes.

In a large nonstick skillet over medium-high heat, warm the olive oil and 1 tablespoon of the butter, swirling to combine, until melted and hot. Dredge the fillets in the flour mixture, coat thoroughly, and tap off the excess. Carefully place each fillet, flesh-side down, in the skillet. Cook until the edges are opaque and bottoms are golden brown, 2 to 3 minutes. Carefully turn the fillets over with a spatula and continue to cook until the second side is golden brown and opaque, 2 to 3 minutes more (if the skillet begins to smoke, adjust the heat to medium). Carefully transfer the fillets to an ovenproof serving platter and keep warm in the oven.

Juice one of the lemon halves and cut the other half into four wedges.

Cut the remaining 4 tablespoons butter into four pieces and melt in a small skillet over medium-high heat. Add the shallot, stirring constantly until the butter is golden brown and fragrant with a nutty aroma, about 2 minutes. Remove from the heat, add the lemon juice, ½ teaspoon salt, and pepper to taste and swirl the pan to combine. Taste and adjust with salt and pepper, if necessary. Pour the browned butter over the fish, sprinkle with the parsley, and serve at once with the lemon wedges.

SERVES 4

¼ cup all-purpose flour

1 teaspoon sweet paprika

Kosher salt and freshly ground black pepper

4 (4-ounce) rainbow trout fillets, skin on, rinsed and dried well

1½ tablespoons olive oil

5 tablespoons unsalted butter

1 lemon, halved

1 shallot, finely chopped

2 tablespoons chopped fresh parsley

Amphail Braised Beef

The Dessarin Valley region of Faerûn offers far more than fertile land and majestic sunsets (and wandering monsters). It's also home to some of the finest cattle farming in all Toril. This succulent, slow-cooked beef chuck roast, inspired by a popular regional recipe that originated with the Oglyntyr family in the village of Amphail, is prepared with cider, pear, and ginger—all of which help to activate the full flavor of the meat.

The ginger offers the dish a pleasing warmth and an unexpected nuance, more than an overt gingery flavor, while the fermented hard pear cider provides a touch of residual sweetness, albeit dry and earthy. Don't fret, if you can't track down hard pear cider (sometimes called "perry"), then apple will do just fine! Roasted sweet potatoes or winter squash make a savory accompaniment and taste wonderful with a ladle or two of sweet au jus.

SERVES 4

3 pounds beef chuck roast, trimmed of excess fat

Kosher salt and freshly ground black pepper

2 tablespoons neutral-tasting oil, such as vegetable, canola, safflower, or grapeseed

5 yellow onions, thickly sliced

1 teaspoon dried thyme, crushed

2 teaspoons ground ginger

1½ tablespoons all-purpose flour

1 cup sparkling hard cider, preferably pear

½ cup low-sodium chicken broth

3 ripe-but-firm Bosc, Bartlett, or Anjou pears, peeled, cored, and cut into 1-inch pieces

¾ teaspoon cider vinegar

¼ cup chopped fresh parsley

Set the beef on a cutting board, dry it with paper towels, tie it into a uniform shape with kitchen twine at 2-inch intervals, and sprinkle generously with salt and pepper.

In a large Dutch oven over medium-high heat, warm 1 tablespoon of the oil until shimmering. Add the beef and cook, undisturbed, until deeply browned on the bottom, 3 to 4 minutes. Turn the beef and continue cooking, until well browned on each of the remaining three sides, 10 to 12 minutes more. Transfer the beef to a large bowl.

Return the pot to medium-high heat, add the remaining 1 tablespoon oil, and warm until shimmering. Add the onions and 1 teaspoon salt and cook, stirring and scraping the bottom of the pot occasionally, until the onions begin to soften and release some liquid, about 4 minutes. Adjust the heat to medium-low and continue cooking for 15 minutes, stirring and scraping the bottom of the pot occasionally and adjusting the heat as necessary to make sure the onions are cooking gently, not scorching. Add the thyme, ginger, and flour and continue to cook, stirring, until the onions are sticky and golden, about 5 minutes more. Add the cider, broth, and ½ teaspoon salt. Stir and scrape the bottom of the pot to loosen and dissolve the browned bits.

Meanwhile, preheat the oven to 300°F with a rack in the lower-middle of the oven.

Nestle the beef into the onions (the onions and accumulated juices should come about three-fourths of the way up the sides of the meat). Cover the pot, transfer it to the oven, and cook for 1 hour 35 minutes. Add the pears, nestling them into the onions, return the pot to the oven, and continue to cook, covered, until the beef is extremely tender (a paring knife should slip easily into the meat) and it registers 200°F on an instant-read thermometer, about 2¼ hours more.

Transfer the beef to a cutting board and, using a large slotted spoon, spoon the onions and pears onto a serving platter; tent loosely with foil to keep warm. Pour the accumulated liquid into a measuring cup and let rest until all the fat rises to the surface, about 10 minutes. Tilt the measuring cup and use a wide, shallow soup spoon to skim the fat off the surface and discard it. Add the vinegar and most of the parsley to the defatted liquid and stir to combine. Taste and adjust the seasoning with salt and pepper, if necessary.

Remove the twine from the beef and cut it against the grain into ½-inch-thick slices (or pull it apart into pieces). Place the meat on the platter with the onions and pears, pour the seasoned juices over the meat, sprinkle with the remaining parsley, and serve.

HOMMLET GOLDEN BROWN ROASTED TURKEY WITH SAUSAGE STUFFING AND DRIPPINGS

What else makes the mouth water but a plump bird roasting on a spit above an open hearth? One particular style of this dish was made famous in the Village of Hommlet, on the far side of Nyr Dyv from the City of Greyhawk, where geese are plentiful in the warmer months and turkeys abundant in the winter. This turkey is served with a chunky gravy made from the bird's juices and brimming with bacon. The sausage stuffing comprises a pan-fried spicy ground pork, seasoned white-bread croutons, finely chopped onions, and small chunks of celery all folded into warm broth. A whole bird can be had in Hommlet for a gold piece, but too much turkey can hit you like a well-timed *sleep* spell, so it's better to stick to the legs.

SERVES 4

STUFFING

¾ pound hearty white sandwich bread (8 to 10 slices), cut into ½-inch cubes (about 8 cups, lightly packed)

4 tablespoons unsalted butter

2 teaspoons neutral-tasting oil, such as vegetable, canola, safflower, or grapeseed

12 ounces fresh sweet Italian pork sausage, casings removed, if necessary

1 yellow onion, chopped

2 celery stalks, trimmed and chopped

Kosher salt and freshly ground black pepper

1 tablespoon minced fresh thyme

1½ teaspoons minced fresh rosemary

1½ cups low-sodium chicken broth

2 eggs

½ cup chopped fresh parsley

MAKE THE STUFFING. Preheat the oven to 250°F with a rack in the middle of the oven. Spread the bread cubes in an even layer on a large rimmed baking sheet and bake until dry and firm, about 45 minutes, stirring them several times. Transfer the bread cubes into a very large bowl and set aside.

MEANWHILE, PREPARE THE TURKEY. Increase oven temperature to 400°F. In a small bowl, mix together 1½ tablespoons salt and 2 teaspoons pepper. Scatter the carrot, celery, and onion in a roasting pan or other stovetop-safe pan into which the drumsticks will fit.

Using your fingers, loosen but do not detach the skin from the drumsticks. Brush about half the melted butter under the skin, sprinkle each with some of the salt and pepper mix, and reposition the skin. Brush the drumsticks' skin with the remaining butter and sprinkle each with some of the remaining salt and pepper mix. Arrange the drumsticks over the vegetables in the pan.

Roast until an instant-read thermometer inserted into the thickest part of each drumstick registers 180° to 185°F, 1 to 1¼ hours. Transfer the drumsticks to a platter, cover loosely with foil, and set aside.

WHILE THE TURKEY ROASTS, FINISH PREPARING THE STUFFING. Grease a broiler-safe 8-inch square (or similarly sized) baking dish with 1 tablespoon of the butter and set aside.

In a skillet over medium-high heat, warm the oil until shimmering. Add the sausage and cook, stirring and breaking up clumps into small crumbles, until some of the fat has rendered and the sausage is lightly browned, about 5 minutes. With a slotted spoon, transfer the sausage to paper towels to drain, leaving the fat in the skillet.

Add the remaining 3 tablespoons butter to the skillet and melt. Add the onion, celery, and ½ teaspoon salt and cook, stirring occasionally, until very soft, 5 to 7 minutes. Add the thyme and rosemary and cook, stirring, until fragrant, about 1 minute. Add ¾ cup of the broth and stir and scrape the bottom of the skillet to loosen any brown bits. Add this mixture, the sausage, 1 teaspoon salt, and pepper to taste to the bowl of bread and toss well to combine. Taste and adjust the seasoning with additional salt and pepper, if necessary.

In a small bowl, whisk the remaining ¾ cup broth and the eggs until well combined. Add the egg mixture and most of the parsley to the bowl of bread mixture and toss to combine well. Pour the stuffing into the prepared baking dish, spread it into an even layer, cover the dish tightly with foil, and place it on a baking sheet. Put in the oven with the turkey and bake until the stuffing is heated through and the moisture from the mixture is bubbling around the edges of the dish, about 50 minutes.

ONCE THE TURKEY IS DONE ROASTING, MAKE THE GRAVY. Use a slotted spoon or skimmer to hold back the solids in the roasting pan and pour the accumulated liquid into a fat separator or measuring cup. Let rest until all the fat rises to the surface, about 10 minutes. If you are using a fat separator, pour the drippings into another container and reserve the fat; if you are using a measuring cup, tilt it and use a wide, shallow soup spoon to skim the fat off the surface and deposit into another container. Reserve the remaining juices.

CONTINUED ON PAGE 18 →

TURKEY

Kosher salt and freshly ground black pepper

1 carrot, peeled and coarsely chopped

1 celery stalk, trimmed and coarsely chopped

1 small yellow onion, coarsely chopped

4 large, bone-in, skin-on turkey drumsticks (about 1 pound each)

3 tablespoons unsalted butter, melted and cooled

GRAVY

2¼ cups low-sodium chicken broth, plus more as needed

6 slices thick-cut bacon

1 carrot, peeled and finely chopped

1 celery stalk, trimmed and finely chopped

1 yellow onion, finely chopped

1 teaspoon minced fresh thyme

3 tablespoons all-purpose flour

1 teaspoon fresh lemon juice

¼ cup finely chopped fresh parsley

Kosher salt and freshly ground black pepper

Hommlet Golden Brown Roasted Turkey with Sausage Stuffing and Drippings,

CONTINUED

Set a strainer over a bowl. Place the roasting pan with the roasted vegetables over medium heat and cook undisturbed, until the vegetables begin to brown and stick to the pan, 3 to 4 minutes. Add 1 cup of the chicken broth and, using a wooden spoon, stir and scrape the bottom of the pan to loosen and dissolve the browned bits. Strain the liquid and discard the solids. Add the reserved juices liquid and enough chicken broth to equal 3 cups and set aside.

Wipe out the pan, set it over medium-low heat, and fry the bacon, turning it over as necessary, until well-rendered and lightly browned, about 13 minutes. Transfer the bacon to paper towels to drain, chop it, and reserve. You should have about 3 tablespoons of fat left in the pan.

Set the pan over medium heat and warm until the fat is shimmering. Add the carrot, celery, onion, and thyme and cook, stirring, until the vegetables soften, about 4 minutes. Add the flour and cook, stirring constantly, until dark golden and fragrant with a nutty aroma, 3 to 4 minutes. Switch to a whisk and, whisking constantly, gradually add the strained broth mixture. Continuing to whisk, cook until the gravy thickens, about 8 minutes. Add the lemon juice, parsley, bacon, and pepper to taste and whisk to combine. Taste and adjust the seasoning with salt and pepper, if necessary.

Once the stuffing is done, if you wish to crisp the skin on the underside of the drumsticks, preheat the broiler. Line a broiler-safe pan or rimmed baking sheet with foil, arrange the drumsticks with the browned sides down, and broil until the skin is browned and crisp, 5 to 7 minutes.

Remove the foil from the stuffing and fluff with a fork. If you'd like to crisp the surface of the stuffing, return the dish to the oven, and broil, checking frequently to prevent burning, until the surface is a shade darker and starting to crisp, 5 to 7 minutes. Sprinkle the stuffing with the remaining parsley. Serve the drumsticks piping hot alongside the stuffing and gravy.

GURDATS

If you love mushrooms and cheese, then this is the dish for you! Gurdats are a cheap and filling side dish prevalent on many a Sword Coast tavern menu. Some of the best examples of this appetizer "in the wild" are found at A Pair of Black Antlers in Elturel, which doesn't shy away from the cheese, or at The Seven-Stringed Harp in Secomber, where the chef goes heavy on the pepper-spice without overpowering the earthy fungal flavors. The version presented below is a classic interpretation of this traveler staple.

Preheat the oven to 425°F with a rack in the middle of the oven. Line a large rimmed baking sheet with foil, set a wire rack in the baking sheet, and coat it with nonstick cooking spray.

In a very large bowl, vigorously whisk together 2 tablespoons of the olive oil, the lemon juice, ½ teaspoon salt, and a few grinds of pepper. Add the mushroom caps and toss gently to coat. Arrange them gill-sides up on the rack and roast until they shrink slightly and fill with liquid, 15 to 18 minutes. Pour off the liquid from the caps, turn them over, and continue roasting until browned and tender, 6 to 10 minutes more. Remove them from the oven and set aside, but leave the oven on.

Meanwhile, in a bowl, whisk together 1 tablespoon olive oil, half the garlic, ½ teaspoon salt, and a few grinds of pepper. Add the breadcrumbs and 2 tablespoons of the parsley, toss until the crumbs are lightly moistened, and set aside.

In a skillet over medium heat, warm the remaining 1 tablespoon olive oil until shimmering. Add the chopped mushroom stems, shallot, thyme, and ½ teaspoon salt. Cook, stirring until the mixture is softened and browned, about 8 minutes. Add the remaining garlic and cook, stirring until fragrant, about 1 minute. Add the sherry and stir, to cook off the alcohol and thicken the mixture slightly, 1 to 2 minutes. Scrape the mixture into a bowl and let cool to room temperature.

Add ⅓ cup of the breadcrumb mixture, the remaining parsley, the Peppadews, Parmesan, cream cheese, ¼ teaspoon salt, and a few grinds of pepper to the bowl and mix until uniform. Taste and adjust the seasoning with additional salt and pepper, if necessary.

Turn the mushroom caps gill-side up and scoop a generous 1 tablespoon of filling into each. Dip the mushrooms filled-side down in the remaining breadcrumb mixture to coat the filling and arrange on the rack. Roast until the filling is hot and the crumb topping is crisp and light golden brown, 15 to 20 minutes. Serve hot.

SERVES 4 TO 6

4 tablespoons extra-virgin olive oil

½ teaspoon fresh lemon juice

Kosher salt and freshly ground black pepper

24 large cremini or white button mushrooms, stems finely chopped, caps left whole

5 garlic cloves, finely chopped

⅔ cup breadcrumbs

½ cup finely chopped fresh parsley

1 shallot, minced

1½ teaspoons minced fresh thyme

¼ cup dry sherry, such as Amontillado

¾ cup finely chopped hot Peppadew peppers, (see Cook's Note)

¾ cup coarsely grated Parmesan cheese

3 tablespoons cream cheese, softened

--- ◆ COOK'S NOTE ◆ ---

With their fruity, tangy, sweet, and spicy flavor notes, Peppadew peppers (a type of pickled pepper, sold in jars) can be found either hot or mild; the hot variety is preferred here. Blot them dry with paper towels before chopping them.

HAND PIES

These palm-size pastries are as near a tavern staple as you can get. From town to town, you can find them stuffed with an astonishing variety of ingredients, ranging from venison or minced chicken to beef, minted lamb, or peacock (though usually just with leftovers from the meal before). Hand pies take on many forms and flavors and travel particularly well, making them adventurer-friendly fare. The variety presented below, made famous at Cuttle's Meat Pies located in Waterdeep's Trades Ward, is flavored with bacon and leeks and is extremely popular across the Heartlands, the Dales, and even the Savage Coast north of Faerûn, where hungry adventurers simply can't get enough of them.

❖

In a large nonstick skillet over medium heat, fry the bacon, turning it over as necessary, until well-rendered and lightly browned, about 13 minutes. Transfer the bacon to paper towels to drain and reserve.

Measure the rendered fat. Reserve 2½ tablespoons and save the rest for another use or discard it. Return 1½ tablespoons of the fat to the skillet, set over medium-high heat, and allow the fat to warm until shimmering. Add the potato and cook, stirring occasionally, until it begins to soften, about 7 minutes. Add the remaining 1 tablespoon bacon fat and allow it to warm until shimmering. Add the leeks, thyme, and ½ teaspoon salt and cook, stirring, until the leeks soften, about 4 minutes. Add the garlic and cook, stirring, until fragrant, about 1 minute. Scrape the mixture into a bowl and set aside.

Wipe out the skillet, return it to medium-high heat, add the beef, and cook, stirring and breaking up any clumps, until it begins to lose its pink color, 4 to 5 minutes. Adjust the heat to medium, add the flour, and cook, stirring constantly, for 1 to 2 minutes. Add the broth and ¾ teaspoon salt and cook, using a wooden spoon to scrape the bottom of the skillet to loosen and dissolve any sticking browned bits, until the mixture thickens (and is almost a bit pasty), about 2 minutes. Scrape the mixture into the bowl with the potato mixture, stir to incorporate the two, and set aside to cool until barely warm, about 20 minutes.

Grumble the bacon and add to the bowl with the parsley; stir to incorporate. Taste and adjust the seasoning with salt and pepper, if necessary. Cover and set aside in the refrigerator.

CONTINUED ON PAGE 22 →

MAKES FOUR 6-INCH HAND PIES

6 slices thick-cut bacon

1 large (about 8 ounces) Yukon gold potato, peeled and cut into ½-inch pieces

2 leeks, white and light green parts, halved lengthwise and thinly sliced

1 tablespoon finely chopped fresh thyme

Kosher salt and freshly ground black pepper

4 garlic cloves, finely chopped

1 pound ground beef

3 tablespoons all-purpose flour

⅔ cup low-sodium chicken broth

¼ cup chopped fresh parsley

Pastry for 2 double-crust pies (about 1½ pounds), thawed if frozen

1 egg

Ketchup, grainy mustard, or steak sauce to serve (optional)

Hand Pies,
CONTINUED

Preheat the oven to 375°F with a rack in the middle of the oven. Line a large rimmed baking sheet with parchment paper or a nonstick (silicone) liner. Have a small bowl of water handy. If working with homemade pie pastry, divide the dough into quarters. On a lightly floured work surface or parchment paper, roll out a quarter of the dough to make rounds.

Cut the dough into a 10 by 8-inch oval. Place 1 cup of the filling mixture on the bottom third of the dough (a narrow end), leaving about a 1½-inch border around the edges. Moisten the whole perimeter of the dough with water and, using a bench scraper if necessary, fold the top of the oval over the filling to form a half-moon shape. Press the dough around the filling to eliminate any air and to seal. Use the tip of a knife to make a small vent in the shape of an "X" in the center of each pie. Trim any ragged edges and, using a fork, crimp the edges to seal them. Again, using a bench scraper if necessary, transfer the formed pie to the prepared baking sheet. Repeat with the remaining pastry and filling.

In a small bowl, beat the egg with 1 tablespoon water and brush the top and sides of each pie with the mixture. Bake until the pies are golden brown and crisp, 40 to 45 minutes, rotating the pan halfway through. Transfer the pies to a wire rack, cool for 5 to 10 minutes, and serve hot with ketchup, grainy mustard, or steak sauce on the side.

Dark Molasses Nutbread

From Silverymoon to Sharn, variations on this classic loaf (sometimes referred to as Amn Blackbread) are plentiful, but most agree that this baked treat is at its best when crafted from the sweetest, strongest molasses in Amn. Traditionally served by the slice, it is slathered with whipped, salted butter—on both sides for the brave! This dense and delicious bread, which accompanies many a main course at inns across the land, is often filling enough to be a meal by itself.

Preheat the oven to 350°F with a rack in the middle of the oven. Butter and flour an 8½ by 4½-inch loaf pan and tap out the excess (or coat with nonstick baking spray).

In a bowl, whisk together the all-purpose flour, rye flour, cornmeal, baking soda, baking powder, and salt. Add the walnuts and stir to distribute.

In another bowl, whisk together the buttermilk, molasses, and melted butter (the butter will clump, which is fine).

Make a well in the center of the dry mixture, add the wet mixture, and, using a flexible spatula, fold and stir until the wet and dry ingredients are just incorporated (do not overmix). Scrape the batter into the prepared pan and smooth the top.

Bake for 40 to 45 minutes, rotating the pan halfway through, until the loaf is firm to the touch, the edges pull away from the pan slightly, and a toothpick inserted into the center comes out clean.

Cool the bread in the pan on a wire rack for 20 minutes. Turn out the loaf, place it right-side up on the rack, and cool to room temperature. To serve, slice with a serrated knife.

MAKES ONE 8½-INCH LOAF

¾ cup all-purpose flour

¾ cup rye flour

¾ cup fine or medium-ground yellow cornmeal

¾ teaspoon baking soda

½ teaspoon baking powder

1 teaspoon kosher salt

1½ cups coarsely chopped toasted walnuts

1 cup buttermilk

½ cup unsulphured molasses (not blackstrap)

¼ cup unsalted butter, melted and cooled

--- ◆ COOK'S NOTE ◆ ---

Rye flour is available from Bob's Red Mill and is sometimes found in the bulk department of a supermarket or natural foods store.

TROLLTIDE CANDIED APPLES

Troll or treat! Held on the first day of every Kythorn, the Trolltide holiday commemorates the City of Waterdeep's victory during the Second Trollwar. Dressed as the pesky troll invaders, children scamper from door to door demanding tasty tributes, such as candies, fruits, and salted meat sticks. Shoppes and homes that come up short are sure to face the consequences at sundown: mischievous pranks that range from late-night troll scratchings at the door to far more insidious missile attacks that involve raw eggs on unprotected entryways, windows, and signs. These delicious candied apples, often carved with silly or spooky troll faces, serve as the perfect ransom to ward off ill-tempered trolls, ensuring peaceful Trolltide evenings for well-prepared Waterdhavians.

MAKES 4 APPLES

4 apples, scrubbed clean and dried well

1¼ cups sugar

3 tablespoons light corn syrup

½ teaspoon red food coloring, plus more as needed (optional)

¼ cup water

¼ teaspoon pure vanilla extract

Line a baking sheet with parchment paper. Working one at a time, spear each apple through the core end and most of the way through the fruit with a Popsicle stick or chopstick. Place the apples on the baking sheet.

In a small saucepan over medium-high heat, combine the sugar, corn syrup, food coloring (if using), and water and bring to a boil, stirring occasionally. Adjust the heat to medium and simmer, swirling the pan occasionally, until the mixture registers between 300° and 310°F on an instant-read, candy, or deep-fry thermometer, 15 to 18 minutes. Add the vanilla near the end of that time.

Working quickly, take the pan off the heat and tilt it to pool the candy mixture on one side. Dip the apples, one at a time, twirling them to coat entirely with the candy mixture. Hold each apple straight over the pot and allow the excess candy mixture to drip off. Return the apples to the parchment paper–lined baking sheet.

Allow the apples to cool, set, and dry for 20 minutes before serving.

◆ COOK'S NOTE ◆

For best results, use hard, tart apples such as Honeycrisp or Granny Smith. Supermarket apples often have a coating to help protect them, so make sure to scrub your apples well and dry them thoroughly.

VEDBREAD

Popularized in Khorvaire's frigid northeastern nation of Karrnath, this savory dinner bread has staved off numerous famines and sometimes served as an all-in-one ration for the country's living soldiers (don't ask what the non-living soldiers eat). Traditionally prepared with sharp, "ved" cheese and presented with onion butter, these crusty buns are best served warm, but can sometimes last for days on the shelf without the use of magical means or preservatives. Unsurprisingly, this tasty staple has migrated to many different worlds, each adding its own local flourish and embracing it as their own. This particular recipe comes from Lorren's Bakery in Faerûn's Village of Red Larch, and features mushrooms and cheese from local, outlying farms. Pair it with some drippings and skewered capons or golden brown roasted turkey (see page 16) from Drouth's Fine Poultry nearby, and you've got yourself a meal.

MAKE THE FILLING. In a food processor, pulse the mushrooms to finely chop, using about eight 1-second pulses.

In a skillet over medium heat, melt the butter. Add the shallots and cook, stirring, until they begin to soften, about 2 minutes. Add the mushrooms and ¼ teaspoon salt, adjust the heat to medium-high, and cook, stirring, until the mushrooms release their liquid and it evaporates fully, 9 to 12 minutes. Add the thyme and cook, stirring, until fragrant, about 1 minute. Remove from the heat, add the Parmesan, and stir to mix. Taste and adjust the seasoning with additional salt and pepper, if necessary. Spread the mixture on a plate and cool to room temperature.

Preheat the oven to 425°F with a rack in the middle of the oven. Line a large rimmed baking sheet with parchment paper or a nonstick (silicone) liner.

MAKE THE DOUGH. In a large bowl, whisk together the flour, baking powder, sugar, and salt. Add the grated Gruyère and whisk to combine.

In a small bowl, whisk the buttermilk and melted butter to combine (the butter will clump, which is fine). Add the buttermilk mixture to the flour mixture. With a sturdy spoon, stir to form a sticky, chunky dough. Turn the dough onto a floured work surface and knead until it holds together and is mostly smooth; do not overknead. Lift the dough and sprinkle more flour underneath it, if necessary, as well as over the surface. Roll or pat the dough into a roughly 12 by 18-inch rectangle; brush any excess flour off the surface.

CONTINUED ON PAGE 28 →

MAKES ABOUT 14 BUNS

FILLING

12 ounces cremini mushrooms, coarsely chopped (see Cook's Note)

2 tablespoons unsalted butter

2 shallots, finely chopped

Kosher salt

1 teaspoon finely chopped fresh thyme

¼ cup freshly grated Parmesan cheese

Freshly ground black pepper

DOUGH

2¼ cups all-purpose flour, plus more for rolling

1 tablespoon baking powder

1 teaspoon sugar

½ teaspoon kosher salt

6 ounces Gruyère cheese, coarsely grated

¾ cup buttermilk, cold

6 tablespoons unsalted butter, melted and cooled

1 egg

Truffle oil for brushing (optional)

Vedbread,

CONTINUED

——— ✦ COOK'S NOTE ✦ ———

You can use an equal quantity of stemmed, coarsely chopped shiitake mushrooms in place of the creminis.

Spread the cooled mushroom filling evenly over the entire surface of the dough; it will be a very thin, patchy layer. With the long side facing you, roll the dough into a very tight, even, compact cylinder. Pinch the seam along the entire length of the cylinder to fasten. Using a serrated knife in a sawing motion, trim off the very ends of the cylinder and discard. Cut the cylinder into 1¼-inch pieces (you should have about fourteen) and arrange them cut-sides up on the baking sheet, about 2 inches apart.

In a small bowl, beat the egg with 1 tablespoon water and brush the top and sides of each bun with the mixture. Bake until the buns are golden brown, about 18 minutes, rotating the pan halfway through.

Cool the buns on the pan for about 5 minutes, then transfer them to a wire rack to cool. Brush with a light coating of truffle oil (if using). Serve warm or at room temperature. Store leftover buns in an airtight container at room temperature and reheat them in a preheated 300°F oven for about 8 minutes before serving.

OTIK'S SKILLET-FRIED SPICED POTATOES

This famous side dish, comprising chopped potatoes, served spiced and fried, is derived from the personal recipe of Otik Sandath, proprietor and chef of the Inn of the Last Home, located in a remote Krynn city called Solace in Ansalon. Otik's personal blend of garlic, paprika, pepper, cayenne, and a sizeable scoop of local salted butter is often emulated but tough to beat; however, the recipe featured below is widely thought to be the closest that one can come to the feeling of sitting atop the famed vallenwood tree tavern with one of his homebrewed dark ales in hand. These potatoes pair well with any braised meats on the menu or with eggs as a day starter.

In a 12- to 14-inch skillet over medium-high heat, warm 1 tablespoon of the oil until shimmering. Add the onion and ½ teaspoon salt and cook, stirring, until softened, about 4 minutes. Adjust the heat to medium and continue cooking, stirring often, until deep golden and some pieces are starting to brown at the edges, 4 to 6 minutes more. Scrape the onion onto a plate and wipe out the skillet.

Meanwhile, put the potatoes in a large microwave-safe bowl, cover, and microwave until the edges of the potatoes begin to soften, 5 to 7 minutes, shaking the bowl to redistribute the potatoes midway through.

Warm the remaining 1 tablespoon oil and the butter in the now-empty skillet over medium-high heat, swirling the pan to combine them. Add the potatoes (leaving behind any liquid accumulated in the bowl) and shake the skillet to coat the potatoes with the fat and evenly distribute them in a single layer, making sure that one side of each piece lies flat on the cooking surface. Cook, undisturbed, until golden brown on the bottom, 6 to 7 minutes. Using a wide spatula, carefully turn the potatoes, taking care not to rip their crusts, and again spread them into a single layer with unbrowned sides lying flat on the cooking surface, and continue cooking, undisturbed, until golden brown on the bottom, about 6 minutes more. Turn the potatoes again and repeat the process until they are tender and well-browned all over, turning one or two more times and adjusting the heat, if necessary, 6 to 12 minutes more. Add ½ teaspoon salt, pepper to taste, the paprika, cayenne, and garlic powder and stir or toss to distribute the seasonings. Add the onion and stir or toss to distribute. Taste and adjust the seasoning with additional salt and pepper, if necessary. Serve hot, sprinkling each serving with the chives.

SERVES 4

2 tablespoons neutral-tasting oil, such as vegetable, canola, safflower, or grapeseed

1 large yellow onion, chopped

Kosher salt

1½ pounds (about 4) Yukon gold potatoes, scrubbed (or peeled if desired), quartered lengthwise, and cut into ¾-inch pieces

1 tablespoon salted butter

Freshly ground black pepper

1 teaspoon sweet paprika

1 teaspoon cayenne

½ teaspoon garlic powder

2 tablespoons minced fresh chives

Yawning Portal Buttermilk Biscuits

These unassuming buttermilk biscuits will melt in your mouth. Rumor has it that the esteemed Lady Alustriel Silverhand provided the Yawning Portal's famed former-adventurer-turned-proprietor, Durnan, with her very own recipe for these savory, flaky cakes, now served by the basket "round the clock." While the inn's undisputed main attraction is the cavernous portal that descends straight into deadly Undermountain dungeon, these famed biscuits are a close second. Whether slathered with a softened rose-apple butter spread or graced with elderberry preserves or brackleberry jam, you can't go wrong with this irresistible quick and easy human staple. And now you can make them in the warm confines of your own humble abode with this coveted recipe. Weary travelers (and excessive drinkers) take note: it is claimed that nothing helps shake off fatigue or an ale-induced hangover quite like one of Durnan's made-to-order morningfeast biscuit sandwiches, composed of easy poached or scrambled eggs and your choice of freshly fried thick-cut ham or pork roll.

Preheat the oven to 450°F with a rack in the middle of the oven. Grease an 8-inch square baking pan (preferably metal) with 1 tablespoon of the room-temperature butter, making sure to grease the corners and edges of the pan.

Coarsely cut the 10 tablespoons chilled butter into ½-inch pieces and refrigerate until needed.

In a bowl, whisk together the flour, baking powder, baking soda, salt, and sugar. Add the chilled butter, toss the pieces in the dry mixture to coat them, and use your fingertips to break up and press the butter into pea-size pieces. Add the buttermilk and, with a sturdy spoon, stir to form a sticky dough with no pockets of dry ingredients remaining. Coat a flexible spatula with nonstick cooking spray and scrape the dough into the greased baking pan. Flour your hands generously and pat the dough into an even layer, making sure to push it into the corners and to the edges. Clean and coat the spatula again, if necessary, and score the dough into nine equal squares (two cuts in each direction, dividing the dough into three rows in each direction), reaching to the bottom of the pan as you score.

Bake until the biscuits are deep golden brown on top, about 30 minutes, rotating the pan 180 degrees halfway through the baking time.

Cool the biscuits in the pan for 5 minutes. Remove the biscuits from the pan and set them on a wire rack. Cut the remaining 1 tablespoon room-temperature butter into ½-inch pieces, put them on the surface of the biscuits, wait a moment for them to begin melting, and use a brush or the spatula to spread evenly over the biscuits. Cool the biscuits for about 12 minutes more, pull them apart, and serve warm.

MAKES ABOUT 9 BISCUITS

12 tablespoons unsalted butter:
2 tablespoons at room temperature,
10 tablespoons chilled

3½ cups all-purpose flour,
plus more for dusting

1½ teaspoons baking powder

½ teaspoon baking soda

1¼ teaspoons kosher salt

1½ teaspoons sugar

1⅔ cups buttermilk, cold

"When they ate breakfast, though, Regis hoped that more information would be forthcoming, for the biscuits that this traveler had given to Drizzt were truly delicious and incredibly refreshing. After only a few bites, the halfling felt as if he had spent a week at rest."

–R.A. SALVATORE,
STREAMS OF SILVER

KARA-TUR NOODLES

Few nations on the planet Toril are as powerful or influential as the human empire of Shou Lung, found in the vast region of Kara-Tur. While this region boasts distinct religions and a proud culture, it also possesses an equally strong culinary tradition. Although there is sparse interaction or conflict between the city-states of the Sword Coast and Kara-Tur, many of its tea leaves, such as Pale Jade, Fim Fim, Dragon's Eye, and Long Jing, are imported in significant quantities by Faerûnian traders, and certain dishes, including various noodles, have made the long migration west as well. While you won't find this stir-fried entrée on just any tavern menu, it has found its way into the more modern eateries of cultural epicenters such as Waterdeep. A heaping bowl of noodles flash-cooked in a deep, oil-drizzled skillet along with chunks of chicken, vegetables, and a salty soy sauce or garum (a fish-based sauce) has become a popular change of pace from the traditional roasts and soups of the Sword Coast.

SERVES 4

3 tablespoons soy sauce

2½ tablespoons Shaoxing rice wine or dry sherry, such as Amontillado

1 tablespoon Asian sesame oil

1 pound skinless, boneless chicken breasts, cut into ½-inch strips

6 ounces dried rice stick noodles (¼ inch wide)

¼ cup plus 2 teaspoons peanut oil or vegetable, canola, safflower, or grapeseed oil

½ cup low-sodium chicken broth

1 teaspoon light brown sugar

½ teaspoon cornstarch

2-inch piece fresh ginger, peeled and finely chopped or grated (about 1½ tablespoons)

5 garlic cloves, finely chopped

¼ teaspoon red pepper flakes, or to taste

In a bowl, whisk together 1 tablespoon of the soy sauce, 1 tablespoon of the rice wine, and 1½ teaspoons of the sesame oil. Add the chicken, toss to coat, cover the bowl, and refrigerate for at least 15 minutes or up to 1 hour.

Meanwhile, put the noodles in a large bowl, cover with boiling water, and stir to separate the noodles. Soak until the noodles are almost tender, about 6 minutes, stirring once halfway through. Drain the noodles, rinse with cold water, and drain again. Return the noodles to the bowl, add 2 teaspoons of the peanut oil, and toss well to coat.

In a small bowl, make the sauce by mixing together the remaining 2 tablespoons soy sauce, remaining 1½ tablespoons rice wine, remaining 1½ teaspoons sesame oil, the broth, brown sugar, and cornstarch; set aside. In another small bowl, mix together the ginger, garlic, red pepper flakes, and 2 teaspoons of the peanut oil; set aside.

In a very large (14-inch) nonstick skillet over high heat, warm 2 teaspoons peanut oil until shimmering. Add half the chicken in a single layer and cook, undisturbed, until the pieces brown on the bottom but are not quite cooked through, about 2 minutes. Transfer the chicken to a large bowl and set aside. Add another 2 teaspoons peanut oil to the skillet over high heat and warm until the oil is shimmering. Add the remaining chicken, cook as before, and transfer to the bowl when finished.

Add another 2 teaspoons peanut oil to the skillet over high heat and warm until the oil is shimmering. Add the onion and cook, stirring occasionally, until the pieces begin to soften and brown at the edges,

2 to 3 minutes; add it to the bowl with the chicken. Add another 2 teaspoons peanut oil to the skillet over high heat and warm until the oil is shimmering. Add the bell pepper and celery and cook, stirring occasionally, until the vegetables are barely tender, 2 to 3 minutes. Adjust the heat to medium, clear the center of the pan, add the remaining 2 teaspoons peanut oil, and allow it to warm until shimmering. Add the ginger-garlic mixture and cook, stirring and mashing it, until fragrant, about 1 minute. Whisk the soy sauce mixture to recombine, add it to the skillet, and cook, stirring and scraping the skillet constantly, until thickened, about 1 minute.

Add the chicken mixture, noodles, all of the scallion whites, and most of the scallion greens to the skillet and toss to combine. Cook, stirring constantly, until the noodles are heated through and coated with sauce, about 2 minutes.

Transfer the mixture to a serving platter, sprinkle with the remaining scallion greens, and serve.

Kosher salt and freshly ground black pepper

1 large yellow onion, halved lengthwise and thickly sliced into slivers

1 large red bell pepper, cored, seeded, and cut into 1-inch squares

1 large celery stalk, cut diagonally into ¾-inch slices

6 scallions, whites thinly sliced and greens cut into 1-inch lengths

---

◆ COOK'S NOTES ◆

A large skillet is important to provide maximum cooking surface for food to spread out. If it is all heaped together, the food will steam instead of achieving the desired browning effect.

Shrimp can be substituted for the chicken. When doing so, buy extra-large (21 to 25 shrimp per pound), and be sure not to overcook them. Cook for 1 to 2 minutes initially, and add them to the vegetable and noodle mixture about halfway through the final heating time, after about 1 minute, so they are only in the mixture until just cooked and heated through, about 1 minute.

Sembian Honey–Glazed Rothé Ribs

Whether you choose beef, pork, or rothé ribs, you can't go wrong with this delightful recipe. Multiple layers of a syrupy, honey-based glaze (the preferred varietal of honey is that of the Faerûnian nation-state of Sembia) are copiously slathered on large racks of ribs, before being delicately roasted over an open flame for careful charring. When prepared properly, this slow-cooked sweet meat falls off the bone easier than the head off an unarmed kobold!

SERVES 4

½ cup ketchup

½ cup honey

1 tablespoon Worcestershire sauce

1 tablespoon cider vinegar

2 teaspoons Dijon mustard

1 tablespoon neutral-tasting oil, such as vegetable, canola, safflower, or grapeseed

1 yellow onion, finely grated

Kosher salt

5 garlic cloves, finely chopped

2 teaspoons chili powder

1 teaspoon smoked paprika

Pinch of cayenne

4½ to 5 pounds baby back ribs, membranes removed, if desired (see Cook's Note)

Freshly ground black pepper

2 scallions, white and light green parts, thinly sliced, for garnish

---

◆ COOK'S NOTE ◆

On the bone (concave) side of the ribs there is a thin membrane that some people prefer to remove. To do so, slit the corner of the membrane with the tip of a paring knife to loosen it. Grab the loose corner with a paper towel (to improve your grip) and pull it up and off. If it doesn't come off in a single sheet, use the paper-towel trick to help pull off the remaining portion.

Preheat the oven to 325°F with a rack in the middle of the oven. Line a large rimmed baking sheet with foil and set a wire rack in the sheet.

In a small bowl, whisk together the ketchup, honey, Worcestershire sauce, vinegar, and mustard until well-blended. Set aside.

In a nonstick skillet over medium heat, warm the oil until shimmering. Add the onion and ½ teaspoon salt and cook, stirring, until the onion appears drier, about 4 minutes. Add the garlic, chili powder, smoked paprika, and cayenne and cook, stirring constantly until fragrant, about 1 minute. Add the ketchup mixture and bring to a simmer, stirring constantly. Continue to simmer, stirring, until the sauce has thickened slightly and the flavors have blended, about 5 minutes. Set aside off the heat to cool briefly; the mixture will thicken as it cools.

Sprinkle both sides of the ribs generously with salt and pepper. Brush about ⅓ cup of the sauce on the bone side, turn the ribs bone-side down, and brush the meaty sides with about ⅔ cup of the remaining sauce. Keeping the ribs bone-side down, roast until the meat is extremely tender (a paring knife should slip easily into the meat) and the meat between the bones in the middle of the racks registers about 205°F on an instant-read thermometer, 2½ to 3 hours; check after 2 hours and cover with foil if the top is getting too dark.

Adjust the oven temperature to 425°F. Brush the remaining ¼ cup sauce on the exposed (meaty) sides of the racks and continue to roast until the sauce heats through but remains sticky, 8 to 10 minutes.

Transfer the ribs to a cutting board and cut as desired. Transfer the cut ribs to a platter, sprinkle with the scallions, and serve hot.

REGHED VENISON POT ROAST

The frozen and unforgiving tundra of Faerûn's North are tested by a brave few and tamed by nearly none. However, the Reghed barbarians, a collection of hardy and superstitious totem-based nomadic tribes, wander the lands with comparable ease, harnessing its sparse potential for the benefit of their relatively small clans. To endure the arduous cold of Icewind Dale, the Reghed and other similar groups, such as the Uthgardt of Northern Faerûn, must maximize time and energy to thrive. Communal meals at winter camps (constructed seasonally to survive the exceptionally long winter) are as central to their dignified warrior culture as their deep religious traditions. Venison (the meat of antelope, deer, or elk) is the most readily available, and thus coveted, finding various uses for these resourceful nomads, but beef or rothé is completely acceptable in other realms. One ceremonial dish (to which the Reghed stake proud claim) that marks the beginning of the long winter is pot roast. A tender flank of beast, chunks of dried apricots, halved gold potatoes, and branches of seasonal herbs intermingle with the natural wild meat juices to make this an especially aromatic and practical single-course meal.

Dry the beef with paper towels, tie it into a uniform shape with kitchen twine at 2-inch intervals, and sprinkle generously with salt and pepper.

In a large Dutch oven over medium-high heat, warm 1 tablespoon of the oil until shimmering. Add the beef and cook, undisturbed, until deeply browned on the bottom, 3 to 4 minutes. Turn the beef a quarter turn and continue cooking, until well browned on each of the remaining three sides, about 10 minutes more; adjust the heat if the bottom of the pot threatens to burn. Transfer the beef to a large bowl.

Return the pot to medium-high heat, add the remaining 1 tablespoon oil, and allow it to warm until shimmering. Add the onion, bay leaves, and 1 teaspoon salt and cook, stirring and scraping the bottom of the pot occasionally, until the onion begins to soften and releases some liquid, about 4 minutes. Add the paprika and flour and continue to cook, stirring, for 2 minutes more. Add the tomato paste and cook, stirring, until fragrant, about 1 minute more.

CONTINUED ON PAGE 38 →

"The reindeer had begun their autumn migration southwest to the sea, yet no human track followed the herd.... In normal barbarian life, the survival of the tribes depended on their following the reindeer herd...."

—R.A. SALVATORE, *THE CRYSTAL SHARD*

SERVES 4

3 pounds beef chuck roast, trimmed of excess fat

Kosher salt and freshly ground black pepper

2 tablespoons neutral-tasting oil, such as vegetable, canola, safflower, or grapeseed

1 large yellow onion, chopped

4 bay leaves

1 teaspoon sweet paprika

1½ tablespoons all-purpose flour

1 tablespoon tomato paste

¾ cup dry white wine

1½ cups low-sodium chicken broth

¾ cup lightly packed dried apricots; ¼ cup finely chopped, ½ cup halved

1 whole head garlic, outermost papery skins removed, top one-quarter of the head cut off to expose the cloves

3 large sprigs fresh thyme

12 ounces carrots, peeled and cut into ¾-inch pieces

12 ounces Yukon gold potatoes, scrubbed or peeled, halved lengthwise, and halves cut into ¾-inch pieces

¼ cup chopped fresh parsley

Reghed
Venison Pot Roast,
CONTINUED

Add the wine to the pot and stir and scrape the bottom to loosen and dissolve the browned bits. Add the broth, finely chopped apricots, garlic, thyme, and ½ teaspoon salt and stir.

Meanwhile, preheat the oven to 300°F with a rack in the lower-middle of the oven.

Nestle the beef (and any accumulated juices) into the pot (the liquid should come about halfway up the sides of the meat). Cover the pot, transfer it to the oven, and cook for 1¾ hours. Then add the carrots, potatoes, and halved apricots, nestling them into the liquid. Cover the pot, return to the oven, and continue to cook until the beef is extremely tender (a paring knife should slip easily into the meat) and it registers 200°F on an instant-read thermometer, 2¼ to 2¾ hours more.

Transfer the beef to a cutting board and, using a large slotted spoon, spoon the carrots, potatoes, onion, and apricot halves to a serving platter; tent loosely with foil to keep warm. Pour the accumulated liquid into a fat separator or measuring cup; remove and discard the bay leaves and thyme sprigs. Reserve the garlic. Let the liquid rest until the fat rises to the surface, about 10 minutes. If using a fat separator, pour the liquid into another container; if using a measuring cup, tilt it and use a wide, shallow soup spoon to skim fat off the surface and discard it (the liquid will be thick, and there may not be much fat at the surface.)

Meanwhile, squeeze the cooked garlic cloves from their skins and mash them to a paste with a fork. Stir the garlic and most of the parsley into the defatted liquid. Taste the gravy and adjust the seasoning with salt and pepper, if necessary.

Remove the twine from the beef and cut it against the grain into ½-inch-thick slices (or pull it apart into pieces) and sprinkle it very lightly with salt and pepper. Place the meat on the platter with the vegetables and apricots, pour the gravy over the meat, sprinkle with the remaining parsley, and serve.

Castle Amber Onion Soup

A rich and hearty soup can be made by following the old recipe of the mysterious d'Amberville family, rogue sorcerers and interdimensional travelers famous for their elaborate banquets. By tradition, the first course would be this onion soup served with peppered croutons and melted Gruyère cheese, usually paired with a mellow amber wine.

While most believe the d'Amberville bloodline to be extinct, it is rumored that on certain nights their spirits return to their ancestral manse, where they will fête adventurers brave enough to dine with the dead. Those who partake of the original dish, fortified with its creator's magic, are said to emerge with heightened resilience!

In a large Dutch oven over medium-high heat, melt 3 tablespoons of the butter. Add the onions and 1 teaspoon salt and cook, stirring occasionally, until softened, about 10 minutes. Adjust the heat to medium, add the bay leaves, and continue cooking, stirring and scraping the bottom of the pot occasionally, until the onions are light gold and sticky, about 1½ hours (adjust the heat as necessary to make sure they are caramelizing, not scorching).

Adjust the heat to medium-low. Add ¼ cup water and scrape the bottom of the pot to loosen and dissolve the brown bits. Continue to cook until the pot bottom is coated again, about 12 minutes, stirring and scraping occasionally. Add another ¼ cup water, and repeat this cooking and deglazing process two more times until all the water has evaporated and the onions are dark brown, about 12 minutes longer each time. Add the thyme and flour and continue to cook, stirring constantly, for about 3 minutes.

Add the sherry to the pot, adjust the heat to medium-high, and continue to cook, stirring and scraping the bottom of the pot constantly, for about 3 minutes longer. Add the chicken broth, beef broth, and 1 teaspoon salt and bring to a simmer, stirring occasionally. Adjust the heat to medium-low and simmer, stirring occasionally, to blend the flavors, about 30 minutes. Remove the bay leaves and stir in the remaining 1 tablespoon butter. Taste and adjust the seasoning with pepper and additional salt, if necessary.

Meanwhile, preheat the oven to 425°F with a rack in the middle of the oven. Arrange the baguette slices on a baking sheet and bake until lightly golden, about 10 minutes, turning them over midway through that time.

Preheat the broiler and carefully set the oven rack about 6 inches below the heat element. Lightly rub each toast with the raw garlic clove; sprinkle with pepper and the Gruyère, and broil until the cheese is melted and browned in spots, about 4 minutes.

Ladle the soup into four warmed bowls, garnish with two cheese toasts each, sprinkle with the chives, and serve at once.

SERVES 4

4 tablespoons unsalted butter

4 pounds (about 8) yellow onions, thinly sliced

Kosher salt

2 bay leaves

1 tablespoon fresh thyme leaves, finely chopped

1 tablespoon all-purpose flour

½ cup dry sherry or dry white wine

4 cups low-sodium chicken broth

1½ cups low-sodium beef broth

Freshly ground black pepper

8 thin slices from a baguette

1 garlic clove, peeled and halved

1¼ cups grated Gruyère cheese

2 tablespoons snipped chives for garnish

Tavern "Steak"

Quick to prepare and highly flavorful, these juicy patties are made of mixed ground meats (both pork and beef or beef and lamb are popular combinations) kneaded together and are chock-full of rich seasonings. Tavern "steaks," as many refer to them, are grilled upon an open flame to help seal in the savory flavors. Often served sans bun with a variety of mild spreads, including fresh creamed dill-yogurt sauce, crushed tomatoes, or a black olive and fig sauce, tavern steaks are a fast dinner option for the hurried tavern hopper.

SERVES 4

DILL-YOGURT SAUCE

¾ cup plain Greek yogurt

2 tablespoons dill pickle relish

2 tablespoons minced shallot

¼ cup finely chopped fresh dill

Kosher salt and freshly ground black pepper

BLACK OLIVE AND FIG SAUCE

6 dried figs, stemmed and quartered

1 cup pitted Niçoise or Kalamata olives, rinsed and drained

1½ tablespoons capers, rinsed, drained, and squeezed dry

2 garlic cloves, finely chopped

1 teaspoon minced fresh thyme

1½ teaspoons fresh lemon juice

2 tablespoons extra-virgin olive oil

Kosher salt (optional)

3 tablespoons chopped fresh parsley

INGREDIENTS CONTINUED →

MAKE THE DILL-YOGURT SAUCE. In a small bowl, whisk together the yogurt, relish, shallot, dill, ½ teaspoon salt, and pepper to taste. Taste and adjust the seasoning with additional salt and pepper, if necessary. Cover and refrigerate until needed.

MAKE THE OLIVE AND FIG SAUCE. In a bowl, cover the figs with 1 cup boiling water and set aside to soften, about 15 minutes. Reserving about ⅓ cup of the soaking water, drain the figs, dry, and finely chop.

In a food processor, combine the olives, capers, garlic, thyme, and lemon juice. Process until finely chopped. With the motor running, slowly add the olive oil. Stop to scrape down the sides of the work bowl and continue pulsing or processing to a desired consistency. Scrape the mixture into a bowl, add the figs, stir, and set aside to blend the flavors, about 15 minutes. Taste and adjust the seasoning by adding salt to taste; adjust the consistency by adding some of the reserved fig soaking liquid, about 1 tablespoon at a time, if necessary. Set the sauce and parsley aside at room temperature.

MAKE THE STEAKS. In a small skillet over medium heat, warm the oil until shimmering. Add the onion and a pinch of salt and cook, stirring, until softened, about 4 minutes. Add the garlic and thyme and cook, stirring, until fragrant, about 1 minute.

CONTINUED ON PAGE 42 →

Tavern "Steak,"
CONTINUED

TAVERN STEAKS

2 teaspoons olive oil

1 small yellow onion, finely chopped

Kosher salt

7 garlic cloves, finely chopped

1½ tablespoons finely chopped fresh thyme

12 ounces ground lamb

12 ounces ground beef chuck

Freshly ground black pepper

◆ COOK'S NOTE ◆

If you choose to serve the tavern steaks with bread, brioche buns or English muffins are excellent options, particularly if you grill them, cut-sides down, while the cooked tavern steaks rest.

In a large bowl, break up the ground lamb and beef into rough chunks. Add the onion mixture, 1½ teaspoons salt, and 1 teaspoon pepper and toss lightly with your hands to distribute the seasonings. Divide the mixture into four 6-ounce portions and, with a light hand, gently form them into patties roughly 4 inches in diameter and 1 inch thick. Press a divot into the top of each patty, if desired. Cover and refrigerate until you are ready to grill.

Prepare a medium-hot fire in a charcoal grill or preheat a gas grill on high for 15 minutes. Clean and oil the grill grate. Grill the patties until grill-marked on the bottom, about 4 minutes. Flip the patties and continue grilling for 3 minutes, until the meat is medium-rare (125° to 130°F on an instant-read thermometer), or for about 6 minutes for medium (135° to 140°F), or for 9 to 10 minutes for well (155° to 160°F).

Transfer the patties to a plate, cover loosely with foil, and let rest for about 3 minutes. Meanwhile, stir the parsley into the olive-fig sauce. Serve the steaks hot with the sauces passed at the table.

GINGERBREAD MAN

A traditional treat served in the waning light of the month of Sunsebb in Greyhawk, this style of gingerbread man memorializes a legend about the ancient ruins of Castle Greyhawk. There, it is said, all sorts of confections could come to life and harry adventurers, including a fearsome cookie whose description inspired this recipe. The arms and legs of the gingerbread man are ringed with icing, but the body is covered in a protective armor of chopped nuts and raisins. Skewering the plumpest raisin could slay the fiend instantly—so a fat raisin is usually reserved for the cookie's mouth. It is customary for children to pluck and eat that one first, to make sure the cookie doesn't come alive!

MAKE THE COOKIES. In a food processor, combine the flour, brown sugar, ginger, cinnamon, baking soda, salt, mustard powder, nutmeg, and cloves. Pulse several times to mix. Add the melted butter, molasses, milk, and vanilla and process until the ingredients are combined into a dough with no remaining streaks of flour, 15 to 30 seconds, stopping to scrape down the sides of the work bowl as necessary.

Dust a work surface very lightly with flour, scrape the dough onto it, and knead briefly until the dough forms a cohesive ball. Divide the dough in half, shape each half into a disk ¾ to 1 inch thick, wrap each one in plastic wrap, and refrigerate for at least 1 hour or up to 24 hours.

Preheat the oven to 350°F with the racks in the upper-middle and lower-middle of the oven. Line two large baking sheets with parchment paper.

Working with one dough disk at a time, roll the dough between two large sheets of parchment paper into a circle about ¼ inch thick; the diameter should be about 11 inches, but the thickness is more important. Make sure the thickness is even from the center to the edges of the circle. Remove the top sheet of parchment and, with a 3½-inch gingerbread man cookie cutter, cut out as many cookies as possible. Peel away the dough scraps and carefully transfer the cut cookies to the prepared baking sheets, arranging them with about 1 inch space around them (about nine per sheet). Mash the dough scraps together and with the remaining refrigerated dough, roll out and cut as many cookies as possible. Not all of the cookies will fit on the two sheets, necessitating a second round of baking. Make sure the cookie sheets cool before loading them with more cookies to bake.

CONTINUED ON PAGE 44 →

MAKES ABOUT 24 COOKIES

COOKIES

3 cups all-purpose flour

¾ cup packed dark brown sugar

1 tablespoon ground ginger

2 teaspoons ground cinnamon

¾ teaspoon baking soda

¾ teaspoon kosher salt

¾ teaspoon dry mustard powder

½ teaspoon freshly grated nutmeg

⅛ teaspoon ground cloves

12 tablespoons unsalted butter, melted and cooled

⅔ cup unsulphured molasses (not blackstrap)

3 tablespoons whole milk

½ teaspoon pure vanilla extract

DECORATION

⅔ cup currants or raisins

⅓ cup very finely chopped toasted walnuts

1⅓ cups confectioners' sugar

1 egg white

¼ teaspoon pure vanilla extract

Kosher salt

Gingerbread Man,

CONTINUED

Bake until the cookies are just set around the edges and slightly puffed, 9 to 11 minutes, rotating the sheets 180 degrees and switching racks midway through the baking. Cool the cookies on the baking sheets for 10 minutes, transfer them to wire racks, and cool completely before decorating.

DECORATE THE COOKIES. Spread the currants on a plate, pick through them to remove any especially large ones, and reserve. In a small bowl, mix ⅓ cup of the tiny currants and the walnuts, and set aside.

With a stand mixer fitted with a whisk attachment, or a handheld electric mixer, beat the confectioners' sugar, egg white, vanilla, a pinch of salt, and 1 teaspoon water on medium-low speed until combined, about 1 minute. Adjust the speed to medium-high and beat until glossy, soft peaks form, 2 to 3 minutes, stopping to scrape down the bowl as necessary.

On each cooled cookie, spread about ½ teaspoon icing around the midriff, as if making a cummerbund. Working quickly while the icing is still tacky, sprinkle a scant 1 teaspoon of the currant-walnut mixture evenly over each cummerbund, pressing it gently to help it adhere.

Scrape the remaining icing into a small sandwich or ziplock plastic bag and, using your hands or a bench scraper, push it into one lower corner of the bag. Cut off 1/16 inch from the very corner of the bag and pipe two eyes and two thin lines of icing on the arms and legs of each cookie. For the mouth, pipe a ¼-inch dot of icing and press a large currant into it. Allow to dry for about 45 minutes. Serve or store in an airtight container for up to 2 days.

"Well met and welcome, traveler, to the Yawning Portal of Waterdeep! They call me Durnan and I'm proprietor of this fine establishment. If you're here for the food and drink, help yourself to a menu. If you need a room, you'll find 'em upstairs. And if you're here to explore the Undermountain, well, traveler, I wish you luck—I was once an adventurer meself, y'know. Entrance and exit through the well will cost you a gold dragon, and payment is always required in advance."

The Yawning Portal
RAINRUN STREET, CASTLE WARD
— SINCE 1306 —

Morningfeast

Eggs and chives	4 cp
Biscuit, ham & egg	3 cp
Porridge and cream	3 cp
Ham platter	4 cp
Talyth	5 cp

Cheeses

Luiren Spring (wheel)	1 sp
Waterdhavian (wheel)	8 cp
Elturian Grey (wedge)	4 cp
Turmish (wedge)	3 cp

Breads

Blackbread and yak butter	6 cp
Onion loaf	4 cp
Buttermilk Biscuits* (basket full)	6 cp
Spiced crabapple butter	1 cp
Dwarven Flatbread with fire lichen spread*	6 cp
Dark Molasses Nutbread*	5 cp

Evenfeast

Melted cheeses*	3 cp
Traveler's stew*	3 cp
Soup, onion & cheese	3 cp
Broth in tankard	1 cp
Cuttle's Hand Pies* (beef)	2 cp
Tavern "Steak"* (pork & beef)	5 cp
Hardbuckler Stew*	7 cp
Quipper, pan-fried	6 cp
Pot Roast with drippings	1 sp
Pheasant, fennel sausage stuffing, gravy	9 cp
Catch of the week, smoked, herb sauce	Market
Prawns and butter sauce	8 cp
Pan-Fried Knucklehead Trout*	Market
Rothé Steak	1 sp
Gurdats*	1 sp
Verbeeg Mutton Stew	7 cp
Harpell Farms Mini Steaks	2 sp
Hot River Crabs	1 sp

Afters

Pear & Roseapple
Cobbler Crumble ....4 cp

Rum pudding ....4 cp

Assorted sweet buns ....3 cp

Pie of the week ....5 cp

Trolltide Candied Apple* ....2 cp

Drinks

Prices by Tankard or Tallglass, and then by Bottle (Hand Keg or "Half-Anker" for Beers)

Mulled Cider ....2 cp • 6 cp

Tavern Punch ....1 cp • 4 cp

Bitter Black Ale ....1 cp • 4 cp

Shadowdark Ale ....2 cp • 6 cp

Stout ....2 cp • 8 cp

Mead ....3 cp • 12 cp

Evermead* ....12 gp • 50 gp

Rollrum* ....2 cp • 8 cp

Clarry ....6 cp • 1 sp

Zzar* ....6 cp • 1 sp

Sherry ....7 cp • 1 sp

Almond Brandy

   Moonshae ....7 cp • 1 sp

   Mintarn ....6 cp • 1 sp

Fruit Liqueurs (apricot, cherry, gooseberry,
peach, pear) ....4 cp • 1 sp

Whiskey ....1 sp • 1 gp

Firewine ....1 gp • 9 gp

Undermountain Aluryath ....5 gp • 2 gp

Arabellan Dry Wine ....2 sp • 8 sp

Saerloonian Glowfire ....2 gp • 12 gp

Winter Wine ....2 sp • 8 sp

Elverquist ....4 gp • 20 gp

Moonlight Knight ....5 gp • 2 gp

Mintwater ....1 cp

Sprucebark Quaff ....3 cp

Tea (pale jade) ....2 cp

Tea (local leaf) ....3 cp

If you don't see what you'd like, ask!

Lodging

Room, standard
includes morningfeast ....1 gp

Room, luxury
includes morningfeast
and evenfeast ....3 gp

The Portal

1 gp per person to descend

1 gp per person to return, placed
in bucket in advance

—Entry is at your own risk—

ELVEN CUISINE

"The elven feast was held in the courtyard just south of the great golden tower. There were no walls about the platform of crystal and marble which sat atop the highest hill in Qualinost, offering an unobstructed view of the glittering city below, the dark forest beyond, and even the deep purple edge of the Tharkadan Mountains far to the south.... Caramon decided he knew why elves were so slender: the food consisted of fruits and vegetables, cooked in delicate sauces, served with bread and cheeses and a very light, spicy wine."

—MARGARET WEIS AND TRACY HICKMAN, *DRAGONS OF AUTUMN TWILIGHT*

E lves have a complicated relationship with their food. As timeless, magical, and ethereal beings who can live for more than 700 years, elves view food as one of the few elements that connects them to mortality. Yet, they love and are ineffably drawn to all good things of the world: nature, magic, art, music, and, of course, food. But not all nourishment is created equal, and elves are especially particular when it comes to what they will put in their bodies. Often seen by outsiders as "picky eaters," their beliefs and life philosophy affect their eating habits every bit as much, if not more so, than their cravings and taste buds.

WHOLESOME AND REFINED

You've probably never seen an elf eat and you probably never will. To be sure, elves will join or even host a supper and the meal in front of them will find a way to disappear over time, but it is rare to ever see an elf actually put a tasty morsel in their mouth. Elves are an intensely private people, and this carries over to every part of their dining. With elves, presentation and etiquette are paramount, and their food is every bit as elegant and graceful as its preparers and consumers. Hand-carved tables adorned with bowls made of marble, gold, and silver set the stage for a visual (and literal) feast of fruits, vegetables, breads, cheeses, and occasional meats—a dream-like display where every imaginable color is represented. Elves pay close attention to what they consume and will not mute the taste with idle banter at the table, apart from giving thanks to their host and the living things that made the meal possible.

TIMELESS TASTES

Perhaps more than any other culture, the tastes, preferences, and palate of the elves are aligned with their lifestyle and firmly rooted in their beliefs. They are a lithe people and the foods they favor are fittingly light, fresh, and wholesome. They generally avoid preservatives and prefer fiber to fat; citrus to salt; and sweet to spicy. Even their iron rations, known as quith-pa, are made up entirely of dried fruits. Because they place such a strong value on life, a high percentage of elves stringently exercise food restrictions, and a great many would fall into the category of vegetarian, vegan, or pescatarian—little that bleeds end up on elven plates. Even with these frequent restrictions, elven culinary mastery is renowned, and many humans who aspire to be gourmet chefs seek apprenticeship among elves.

It is said that all elven subcultures are offshoots of the nomadic high elves who searched the worlds far and wide, choosing to settle in the lands that struck their fancy. Yet, elves are among the most diverse within the multiverse, with cultural variations playing a huge part of that diversity. High elves, such as Eladrin, Qualinesti, and Silvanesti, are the most refined, and insist on the finest-quality ingredients and visual perfection in their feasts. Because these communities are typically insulated and prosperous, they can afford to be choosier in their diets, even introducing complex yet wholesome sauces and garnishes to their dishes. High elves tend to align their diets most closely to their values, and prefer fruits, vegetables, and grains to meat and poultry. By contrast, wood elves are often wanderers and adventurers and, consequently, more disposed to hunting and foraging. These elves necessarily exhibit more flexibility in their diets, ranging from nuts and berries to wild game such as venison, turkey, and rabbit, and fish including salmon and trout. Wood elves also favor consuming whole foods, and relish individual ingredients from the land rather than blending different flavors.

While most differences between elves are somewhat superficial, relegated to simple variations in dress, dwellings, culture, or beliefs, there are two notable exceptions that could almost be categorized as separate groups entirely: half-elves and drow.

While half-elves are technically uncommon, their palate is effectively a blend of elven and human sensibilities. The environment in which half-elves are raised and reside ultimately determines where they fall on the culinary scale, but they typically build their diets with an elven base and venture into human accents and preparation techniques.

Surface-dwelling elves and drow of the Underdark are as different as day and night, especially when it comes to their palates. However, one thing they share in common is a penchant for locally sourced, fresh (sometimes alive, in the case of the drow) ingredients. But unlike the forests of their cousins, the drow's Underdark is a veritable cornucopia of briny, sour, earthy, bitter, and tangy ingredients, from roots and worms to lurkers and fungi. Due to a low supply of salt in the Underdark, vinegars and acids flavor many dishes of the drow, who have as much affinity for meat and fish as they do produce, which for them consists mostly of fungi and tubers.

CULINARY EXPLORATION AND ADVENTURE

Like most cultures of the multiverse, elves prefer to use ingredients sourced from their immediate environment. Elves are primarily gatherers and farmers; although, thanks to their ready access to magic, they cultivate food for subsistence without having to clear or plow lands. Some secret ingredients used in the highest elven cuisine are themselves transmuted through sorcery from mundane plant products and spices such as paprika. The elves that hunt do so thoughtfully, careful not to disrupt the delicate balance of nature.

With regards to beverages, elves largely subsist on sparkling waters from mountain springs, but are known to enjoy spirits and wines, preferring feywine to all other concoctions. This ancient nectar—crafted from flower juice and honey, and imbued with a secret ingredient (one that remains a mystery to humans, dwarves, and even most elves)—is the drink of choice at the majority of elven festivals, providing euphoric effects that can last for days or even weeks. Adventurers be warned—the effects of this drink are powerful and disorienting, often causing members of other groups who imbibe to lose all sense of self for months, which is why elves rarely, if ever, part with it.

Quith-pa

While it may not sate a halfling-size appetite, quith-pa has sustained the bodies of elven adventurers for generations. The most common variety of elven iron rations, this vegetarian trail food is made up primarily of dried fruits, but regional variations can include seeds, nuts, legumes, and beyond. Designed to be as light in the pack as it is in the body, this basic nourishment ensures travelers won't suffer a post-meal slog on the trail. Meanwhile, its wholesome ingredients and simple, clean flavors are perfect for even the most finicky elven palate.

Using a Microplane, grate the orange peel to yield 1½ teaspoons of finely grated zest. Squeeze the orange to yield 1½ tablespoons of juice.

In a full-size or mini food processor, combine the apricots, ¼ cup of the coconut, the orange zest and juice, vanilla, and a tiny pinch of salt. Process until the mixture is very finely chopped, uniform, and cohesive, pulsing and stopping to scrape down the sides of the work bowl as necessary. Scrape the mixture into a small bowl. Put the remaining ½ cup coconut in a wide, shallow bowl.

Roll scant 1-tablespoon portions of the apricot mixture into 1-inch balls, gently pressing as you roll to help them cohere (you should have 15 or 16 balls). Working with three or four balls at a time, roll them in the remaining coconut, pressing them gently to help the coconut adhere. Place the balls on a plate and rest them (to firm up and dry out slightly) for 45 minutes. The balls will keep, stored in an airtight container at room temperature, for about 3 days.

MAKES 15 OR 16 BALLS

1 orange

6 ounces (1 cup) dried apricots, coarsely chopped

¾ cup unsweetened shredded coconut, toasted

¾ teaspoon pure vanilla extract

Kosher salt

> "'What's this junk?' he asked.
>
> 'Quith-pa,' said Gilthanas. 'Iron rations, in your language. It will last us for many weeks, if need be.'
>
> 'It looks like dried fruit!' Caramon said in disgust.
>
> 'That's what it is,' Tanis replied, grinning."
>
> —MARGARET WEIS AND TRACY HICKMAN, *DRAGONS OF AUTUMN TWILIGHT*

Feywild Eggs

There is a parallel plane to the "Prime" (the one that contains all known worlds of the multiverse) known as the Feywild, or the Plane of Faerie, from which sylvan creatures such as pixies, satyrs, unicorns, dryads, and the like originated. It was in this mirror realm, bathed in eternal twilight and ethereal luminescence, that all elven-kind was birthed from swirling, limitless magic, including the eladrin—elves with an unfathomably deep connection to the seasons. These elves, who still call the fey dimension home, boast a highly intuitive link with nature and are able to craft incredible meals with near-perfect combinations of ingredients. One dish, known as Feywild eggs, is a delightful presentation of creamed, herbed, and fluffed eggs, completed over even heat for a golden crisp finish. Some have claimed this simple recipe descended from the leShay, an immortal breed of fey "elves" with incredible, godlike powers. Thankfully, you don't need to visit the Feywild to try these eggs. An elf of good repute has vouched that this concoction is fairly authentic eladrin eating.

SERVES 4

9 eggs

¼ cup freshly grated Parmesan cheese

⅓ cup finely chopped mixed fresh herbs, such as parsley, basil, dill, mint, tarragon, lovage, or celery leaves

½ teaspoon kosher salt

Freshly ground black pepper

2 tablespoons extra-virgin olive oil

1 yellow onion, finely chopped

5 ounces Fontina, Colby, Monterey Jack, Havarti, or Gouda cheese, finely diced (about ½ cup)

Preheat the oven to 400°F with a rack in the middle of the oven.

In a bowl, beat together the eggs, Parmesan cheese, herbs, salt, and a few grinds of pepper until uniformly blended.

In a 10-inch nonstick, oven-safe skillet over medium-high heat, warm the olive oil until shimmering. Add the onion and cook until softened, about 3 minutes. Pour in the egg mixture and cook undisturbed until the edges begin to set and bubbles begin to appear in the center, about 1 minute. Sprinkle the diced cheese evenly over the eggs, transfer the skillet to the oven, and bake until the center is set and the frittata has puffed, about 14 minutes.

Gently run a flexible nonstick spatula around the edges of the frittata to loosen it and ease it onto a serving plate. Let cool for about 15 minutes, cut into wedges, and serve warm or at room temperature.

COOK'S NOTES

Feywild eggs take well to all sorts of additions, including vegetables such as sautéed bell peppers, sliced mushrooms, asparagus, zucchini, or scallions, and meats such as crumbled cooked bacon, thinly sliced or crumbled cooked sausage, or sautéed diced ham steak. Whichever ingredients are added, use no more than 2 cups and make sure they are cooked and seasoned in the skillet before adding the eggs.

Make sure the skillet you choose is oven-safe to 400°F.

High Harvest Puree

Highharvestide is a regional celebration of harvest and plenty that occurs annually near the autumnal equinox in certain regions of Toril. In days past, tradition mandated that elves solely consume nature's dew in honor of giving thanks; however, in recent years, the holiday has evolved into a multicourse feast anchored by a cornucopia of autumnal-themed dishes, including a warm and comforting blend of crop plants. This nourishing puree, a favorite of wood elves and eladrin alike, is a mélange of butternut squash, garlic, and thyme that is slow-simmered for a sweet and earthy flavor and garnished with an olive oil accent.

Preheat the oven to 425°F with a rack in the middle of the oven.

In a large bowl, toss the squash and garlic cloves with the olive oil. Add ¾ teaspoon salt and a few grinds of pepper and toss to distribute. On a large rimmed baking sheet, spread out the squash into a single layer and roast until tender, about 30 minutes. Sprinkle the thyme over the squash, stir it in, and continue to roast for 10 minutes more. Set the baking sheet on a stable, heatproof surface.

Slip the peels off the garlic cloves; discard the peels and return the cloves to the squash. With a potato masher, mash the squash to a desired texture. Taste and adjust the seasoning with salt and pepper, if necessary. Scrape the puree into a serving bowl, drizzle with olive oil, and serve.

SERVES 4

One 4-pound butternut squash, peeled, seeded, and cut into 1-inch cubes

4 large garlic cloves, unpeeled

3 tablespoons extra-virgin olive oil, plus more for drizzling

Kosher salt and freshly ground black pepper

1½ teaspoons finely chopped fresh thyme

COOK'S NOTE

Mashing the squash right on the baking sheet yields a dense, rustic puree. If you want to make it smooth, scrape the squash and peeled garlic into a food processor and pulse or process it to a desired smoothness. If you want a looser consistency, with the processor running, gradually add ½ to ⅔ cup of hot water through the feed tube.

ELVEN BREAD

Elven bakers have protected the secret of this bread for millennia. Both nutritious and delicious, a single bite of this mysterious rolled pastry loaf can sustain an adventurer for a day or more of journeying. Sweet and robust in flavor and made of fine grains and rich butter, elven bread is rumored to boast twice the nutritional value of iron rations at only half the weight, making it essential adventuring fare for elves on the go. Even the most discerning high elves can't resist this wholesome, cinnamon—and sometimes cardamom—swirled treat.

MAKES TWO 8½-INCH LOAVES

DOUGH

2 packages (¼ ounce each) active dry yeast

1½ cups whole milk, lukewarm (110° to 115°F)

½ cup honey

2 eggs, beaten, plus 1 egg for egg wash

¼ cup unsalted butter, melted

2 teaspoons kosher salt

1 cup whole-wheat flour

5 cups all-purpose flour, plus more for rolling

FILLING

½ cup sugar

1 tablespoon all-purpose flour

1 tablespoon ground cinnamon

COOK'S NOTES

Brush the bread with an egg wash before sprinkling on the filling—the egg wash prevents any gaps from forming in the swirl while the bread bakes.

This bread works great as a midday snack, a post-dinner treat, or toasted and buttered for breakfast.

If you prefer more of a dessert bread, double the quantity of cinnamon-sugar filling.

MAKE THE DOUGH. In the bowl of a stand mixer fitted with the paddle attachment, dissolve the yeast in ¼ cup of the lukewarm milk. Add the remaining 1¼ cups milk, the honey, the 2 beaten eggs, the butter, salt, whole-wheat flour, and all-purpose flour. Mix until well combined. Switch to the dough hook attachment and mix on low speed until the dough is elastic and somewhat sticky, about 8 minutes. Alternatively, you can mix and knead the dough by hand on a work surface for about 15 minutes; it's okay if it feels a little sticky.

Put the dough in a lightly greased large bowl, flipping the dough once to grease the top and bottom. Cover with a clean kitchen towel or plastic wrap and set aside in a warm place to rise until doubled in size, about 1 hour.

WHILE THE DOUGH IS RISING, MAKE THE FILLING. Combine the sugar, flour, and cinnamon in a small bowl. Set aside.

In a separate bowl, beat the remaining egg with 1 tablespoon water to make an egg wash.

Generously butter two 8½ by 4½-inch loaf pans. Transfer the dough to a floured work surface, divide in half, and roll one piece into a 6 by 20-inch rectangle. Brush the dough with the egg wash, then evenly sprinkle with the cinnamon-sugar filling. Starting with one of the short sides, roll the dough into a log. Repeat with the remaining dough, egg wash, and filling. Place the logs, seam-sides down, in the prepared loaf pans. Cover and set aside in a warm place to rise until the center of the dough has crested about 1 inch over the rim of the pan, 1½ to 2 hours.

Fifteen minutes before the dough is ready to bake, preheat the oven to 400°F with a rack in the middle of the oven.

Bake for 10 minutes, then lower the oven temperature to 350°F and bake until the loaves are golden brown and sound hollow when tapped, 25 to 30 minutes. Remove the loaves from the pans and let cool completely on a wire rack before slicing.

WOOD ELF FOREST SALAD

This colorful, flower-infused wild-leaf medley with vibrant citrus accents is a quintessential salad of the Kagonesti elves of Krynn. These ancient elves harbor a deep reverence for nature and a refined, almost instinctual, tongue when it comes to culinary combinations. Sometimes called "chopforest" among the wood elves of Toril and Oerth, this bountiful, verdant mix is brimming with sharp accents and crisp textures that almost magically share the palate with the subtler foraged flavors at play. It's as much a visual trip through Ansalon's western woods, from the forest floor all the way to the highest-reaching branches, as it is an edible one.

Finely grate 1 teaspoon of zest from both the orange and the lemon. Transfer the zest to a large salad bowl. Squeeze 2 teaspoons of juice from the lemon and add it to the bowl along with the vinegar, honey, ½ teaspoon salt, and pepper to taste and whisk to combine. Add the shallot and set aside for the flavors to blend, about 10 minutes.

While whisking vigorously, add the olive oil to the bowl in a slow, steady stream to combine and emulsify the dressing. Taste and adjust the seasoning with additional salt and pepper, if necessary. Add the brussels sprouts, toss to coat with the dressing, and set aside for them to begin to soften, about 30 minutes.

Meanwhile, peel the orange, trim away any residual bits of pith, thinly slice the fruit, and cut the slices into quarters.

Add the radicchio and the chives to the sprouts, toss to combine. Add the orange pieces and toss lightly to distribute. Taste and adjust the seasoning with additional salt and pepper, if necessary. Sprinkle the edible flowers (if using) over the salad and serve.

SERVES 4 TO 6

1 orange

1 lemon

1 tablespoon cider vinegar

1 tablespoon honey

Kosher salt and freshly ground black pepper

1 small shallot, finely chopped

¼ cup extra-virgin olive oil

1 pound brussels sprouts, trimmed, halved, and very thinly sliced

½ small head radicchio, thinly sliced; long strands cut in half, if necessary

1 bundle fresh chives, chopped (about ¾ cup), or fresh dill

Edible flowers, such as nasturtiums or pansies, for sprinkling (optional)

ELVEN MARRUTH

These two-bite, turnover-style pastries, stuffed with a variety of minced regional vegetables, are perfect for snacking trailside or at the banquet table. Sometimes reductively referred to as "root pies" by dwarves and humans, marruth are incredibly hearty closed-face canapés that are filled with spiced and herbed mashes of vegetables (cabbage, potatoes, and carrots) and then lightly baked in a flaky, buttery crust. They are traditionally served warm, occasionally as a meal in itself, with a chilled flute of elverquist to wash them down. Once cooled, these pastries can be rolled into rallow leaves (thick and oily waterproof broadleaves) to preserve them for travel.

MAKES ABOUT 12 PASTRIES

1 small yellow onion, finely chopped

1 small Yukon gold potato, peeled and cut into ½-inch pieces

2 carrots, peeled and finely chopped

2 cups packed finely chopped green cabbage

3 tablespoons extra-virgin olive oil

Kosher salt and freshly ground black pepper

2 teaspoons finely chopped fresh thyme, plus 1½ tablespoons picked whole thyme leaves

¾ teaspoon soy sauce

¼ cup chopped fresh dill

All-purpose flour for dusting

Pastry for 2 double-crust pies (about 1½ pounds), thawed if frozen

1 egg

Preheat the oven to 375°F with the racks in the upper-middle and lower-middle of the oven. Line two large rimmed baking sheets with parchment paper or nonstick (silicone) liners.

In a bowl, combine the onion, potato, carrots, cabbage, and olive oil and toss to coat the vegetables with the oil. Add ½ teaspoon salt and a few grinds of pepper and toss to distribute. Transfer the mixture to one of the prepared baking sheets, spreading it into a thin, even layer (set the bowl aside).

Roast the vegetables on either rack until tender, 25 to 30 minutes, stirring and turning the vegetables two or three times. Remove the baking sheet from the oven, add the chopped thyme, and stir to incorporate it. Spread out the mixture and allow to cool to room temperature for about 20 minutes. Leave the oven on for more baking.

Return the cooled vegetables to the now-empty bowl. Stir in the soy sauce, dill, ¾ teaspoon salt, and pepper to taste. Adjust the seasoning, if necessary, and set aside until needed.

Replace the parchment paper on the baking sheet or wash the nonstick liner and return it to the baking sheet. Have a small bowl of water handy.

Dust a large sheet of parchment paper with flour. If you are working with homemade pie pastry, divide the dough into two balls. Working with one ball of homemade pastry, or one sheet of store-bought pastry, roll the dough into a 12-inch circle. Sprinkle half of the whole thyme leaves evenly over the pastry, cover with another sheet of parchment paper, and roll lightly to help the thyme stick. Flip the pastry over so the thyme leaves are on the bottom, and set aside. Repeat with the remaining pastry and remaining whole thyme leaves.

With a 4-inch round biscuit or cookie cutter, cut six circles out of each pastry round, patching together scraps if necessary, for a total of twelve circles. Working with six of the pastry circles, place about 1½ tablespoons of the vegetable mixture in the center of each round, leaving a ½-inch border around the edge. Working with one piece of pastry at a time, moisten the edge of the pastry circle and fold the pastry over the filling to make a half-moon shape. Press out any trapped air, press the edges firmly to seal, and, using a fork, crimp the edges for decoration and to secure the seal. Repeat with the remaining pastry rounds and filling, and transfer onto the prepared baking sheets.

In a small bowl, beat the egg with 1 tablespoon water and brush the top and sides of each marruth with the mixture. Bake until the marruths are light golden brown and crisp, about 25 minutes, rotating the sheets 180 degrees and switching racks halfway through the baking. Set the baking sheets on wire racks, cool the pastries for about 5 minutes, and serve hot.

Drow Mushroom Steaks

A delicacy of the great Underdark City of Spiders, Menzoberranzan, these seasoned ripplebark mushroom steaks are harvested fresh from the fungi fields near Lake Donigarten. While their exact agronomy is a closely guarded drow secret, many speculate that fertilizer from the Donigarten island rothé make these mushrooms grow unusually large, meaty, and nutrient rich. They're so tasty and chewy, you'll think you are eating unicorn! This dish has become so popular that it has migrated to the surface, and it's even rumored to be a favorite of Xanathar of Waterdeep, a notorious beholder who prefers it to surface-grown mushrooms as well as raw meat. But make sure to carefully read the label on that bottle of balsamic vinegar—the drow are as famous for their poisons as their sauces.

In a shallow dish wide enough to hold the mushrooms in a single layer, whisk together the olive oil, lemon juice, balsamic vinegar, thyme, salt, and several grinds of pepper. Put the mushrooms in the dish. Set aside to marinate at room temperature for 15 minutes, turning the mushrooms over and spooning the marinade on them halfway through.

Heat an outdoor grill or indoor grill pan over medium-high heat. Grill the mushrooms, flipping to cook both sides, until tender and browned, 10 to 12 minutes. Serve hot or at room temperature.

SERVES 6

3 tablespoons olive oil

2 tablespoons fresh lemon juice

2 tablespoons balsamic vinegar

1 tablespoon fresh thyme leaves

½ teaspoon kosher salt

Freshly ground black pepper

**6 large portobello mushrooms caps
(stems removed and discarded)**

Cherrybread

In some worlds of the multiverse, this dense dessert bread is also named "fruitcake." Regardless of title or origin, cherrybread boasts various diced bits including dried fruits (cherries, dates, citron, currants, raisins, and sometimes more) marinated in spirits and nuts (walnuts and hazelnuts), all held together by just enough vanilla batter (with a splash of molasses) to do the job. It is sold in bake shoppes the Realms over as small loaf cakes or as leaf-wrapped slices suitable for travel. While this treat surges in popularity during the holidays, cherrybread makes a wonderful addition to teatimes on or off the trail all year long.

MAKES ONE 9-INCH LOAF

¾ cup golden raisins

2 tablespoons dark or amber rum

¾ cup all-purpose flour

½ teaspoon baking powder

¼ teaspoon baking soda

Kosher salt

⅓ cup packed light brown sugar

1⅓ cups packed dried apricot halves

¾ cup dried cherries or cranberries

3 cups walnut halves, lightly toasted and cooled

3 eggs

2 tablespoons unsulphured molasses (not blackstrap)

½ teaspoon pure vanilla extract

COOK'S NOTE

If you vary the type of dried fruit used, cut larger ones, like dates or figs, into smaller pieces. Make sure to include cherries or cranberries for the tart edge to their sweetness. This bread is an excellent accompaniment to a cheese platter.

In a small microwave-safe bowl, combine the raisins and rum, cover, and microwave until warm, about 1 minute. Set the bowl aside, still covered, until the raisins absorb most of the rum and soften, about 1 hour, stirring once or twice during that time. Drain off any excess liquid.

Preheat the oven to 300°F with a rack in the middle of the oven. Butter a 9 by 5-inch loaf pan. Fold two long sheets of parchment paper and lay one crosswise in the pan and lay one lengthwise, pushing the parchment paper into the corners and smoothing the paper so it lies flush in the pan, with the ends overhanging all four sides of the pan. Generously butter the parchment paper in the pan.

In a large bowl, whisk together the flour, baking powder, baking soda, ½ teaspoon salt, and the brown sugar (make sure to break up any lumps in the brown sugar). Add the apricots, cherries, and raisins and toss to coat well. Add the walnuts and toss to combine.

In a small bowl, beat together the eggs, molasses, and vanilla until well blended. Add to the fruit-nut mixture and, using a flexible spatula, fold and mix to combine and coat all the dried fruit and nut pieces with batter (make sure there are no pockets of dry ingredients left at the bottom of the bowl). Scrape the mixture into the prepared pan and smooth it into an even, compact layer.

Bake for about 1 hour, rotating the pan 180 degrees halfway through. If, at that time, the top is browning too much, tent loosely with foil. When the cake is a deep golden brown, transfer the pan to a wire rack and cool completely.

Grab the parchment paper overhangs and remove the loaf from the pan. With a serrated knife, cut it into thin slices, and serve. Leftovers can be wrapped well and stored in an airtight container at room temperature for about 1 week.

GREENSPEAR BUNDLES IN BACON

Greenspear, also referred to as asparagus or "sparrow grass" by humans, is a perennial flower plant that has ascended to staple-status in many elven diets. While elves consume greenspear raw, seasoned, roasted, or steamed with herbs, their half-elf brethren—liberated from certain culinary taboos—have developed an additional preparation technique. In an irreverent touch, but one that flavorfully complements the greenspear, half-elves add salted and cured pork into the mix, in deference to their half-human taste buds. Regarding bacon, the thicker cut is always the better!

Preheat the oven to 425°F with a rack in the middle of the oven.

In a large bowl, toss the asparagus with the olive oil to coat. Sprinkle the asparagus very lightly with salt and pepper and toss again.

Put one slice of bacon on the work surface, lay four asparagus spears on it diagonally, and wrap the bacon around the asparagus, covering as much of the spears as possible and making sure the ends overlap; gently press the ends together to help them adhere. Working in groups of four asparagus spears, repeat with the remaining bacon slices and asparagus to form seven additional bundles.

On a large rimmed baking sheet, arrange the bundles, seam-side down, with about 1 inch of space around them. Roast until the bacon and asparagus are cooked through and spotted brown, about 15 minutes.

Transfer the bundles to a serving platter, sprinkle with the chives, and serve at once.

SERVES 4

2 pounds (about 32) medium-thick asparagus spears, tough ends snapped off

1 tablespoon extra-virgin olive oil

Kosher salt and freshly ground black pepper

8 slices bacon

1½ tablespoons finely chopped fresh chives for garnish

COOK'S NOTES

When choosing asparagus, seek spears that are about ¾ inch thick at the base—about as thick as a highlighter; they will overcook if they are too slender (like a pencil).

If you prefer crispier bacon, use standard-cut instead of thick-cut bacon.

Moonshae Seafood Rice

Originated in the mythical elven isle of Evermeet but popularized by adventurous expatriates along the Sword Coast and its scattered archipelago, this creamy fish rice dish requires a patient chef . . . but it's well worth the wait! Short-grain rice (which yields a stickier, compact texture), along with a medley of ocean "fruits," including shrimp and scallops, is slow cooked in a rich seafood broth until it reaches a smooth, velvety consistency. Butter, onion, saffron, elven dry white wine, and olive oil all intermingle and do their part in activating the dreamy maritime flavors. Some elven chefs of old would finish the dish with a swirl of mascarpone.

SERVES 4

4 cups fish or seafood stock

¼ teaspoon crushed saffron threads

2 tablespoons extra-virgin olive oil

1 onion, finely chopped

Kosher salt

1½ cups Arborio rice

¾ cup dry white wine, at room temperature

12 ounces shelled, deveined extra-large shrimp (21 to 25 shrimp per pound), halved lengthwise

12 ounces dry sea scallops, halved lengthwise

2 tablespoons unsalted butter

3 tablespoons minced chives for garnish

COOK'S NOTES

The exact volume of liquid required for the rice to fully cook can vary. Occasionally, the quantity falls a bit short of the 4 cups in the recipe, but sometimes it takes the full amount.

Note that you have to keep the broth warm while you prepare the rice.

In a small saucepan over medium heat, bring the stock to a simmer. Adjust the heat to low and keep warm. In a small bowl, mix together about ½ cup of the warm stock and the saffron, stirring until the liquid is tinted, and set aside.

In a large saucepan over medium heat, warm the oil until shimmering. Add the onion and ½ teaspoon salt and cook, stirring frequently, until softened, about 4 minutes. Add the rice and cook, stirring constantly, until the edges of the grains begin to turn translucent, 2 to 3 minutes. Add the wine, adjust the heat to medium-low, and cook, stirring frequently, until the wine is absorbed into the rice, about 2 minutes. Add 1 cup of the warm stock and cook, stirring frequently, until it is absorbed into the rice, about 5 minutes. Repeat the process twice more, adding 1 cup stock each time.

Sprinkle the shrimp and scallops lightly with salt, add them to the rice, and continue to cook, stirring occasionally, for 2 minutes. Add the reserved saffron-stock and continue to cook, stirring frequently, until it is absorbed and the rice is fragrant and tinted and appears moist and creamy, about 3 minutes more. The rice grains should be al dente—cooked through, but still with a touch of resistance to the bite—and the shrimp and scallops should be just cooked through and opaque. Add the butter and stir to melt and incorporate. Taste and adjust the seasoning with additional salt. Adjust the consistency with additional stock, if necessary, stirring until it is incorporated. Serve hot, sprinkling each portion with some of the chives.

Dragon Salmon

Aundair is the breadbasket of Eberron's Khorvaire, and the Aundair River is famous for the seafood that half-elven anglers bring back to the markets of Fairhaven. Their traditional preparation of the enormous salmon that spawn in that river, like much else in Aundair, relies heavily on sauces: in this case a butter and dark wine reduction. The aristocracy would sample only a tiny fillet before moving on to further courses, but in simpler households, a single dragon salmon could feed a family. After their fish, the locals would turn to a cremfel, a thin pancake stuffed with rich cream and slices of fresh fruit.

Preheat the oven to 200°F with a rack in the middle of the oven.

Sprinkle the salmon lightly with salt and pepper.

In a large nonstick skillet over medium-high heat, warm the oil until shimmering. Add the salmon flesh-side down, leaving at least ¼ inch of space around the pieces, and cook, undisturbed, until the bottoms of the fillets start to turn opaque, 3 to 4 minutes. Gently flip the fillets skin-side down, and cook, again undisturbed, until they are no longer translucent on the exterior and are firm when gently pressed, about 3 minutes for rare or 4 minutes for medium. Transfer the salmon to a heatproof plate, tent loosely with foil, and place it in the oven to keep warm.

Wipe out the skillet, add 1 tablespoon of the butter, and melt it over medium-low heat. Add the shallot, thyme, and ¼ teaspoon salt and cook, stirring constantly, until the shallot softens, about 1 minute. Add the wine and broth, adjust the heat to medium-high, and bring the mixture to a simmer, occasionally stirring and scraping the bottom of the skillet to loosen and dissolve any browned bits. Continue simmering until reduced by about two-thirds, 6 to 8 minutes longer, adding any accumulated salmon juices midway through. Adjust the heat to low, add the remaining 1 tablespoon butter, ¼ teaspoon salt, and pepper to taste. And stir constantly while the butter melts and incorporates into the sauce. Taste and adjust the seasoning with additional salt, if necessary. Pour or spoon the sauce over or around the salmon, sprinkle with the chives, and serve hot.

SERVES 4

1½ pounds skin-on salmon fillet, pinbones removed if necessary, cut crosswise into 4 equal pieces, and blotted dry

Kosher salt and freshly ground black pepper

2 tablespoons neutral-tasting oil, such as vegetable, canola, safflower, or grapeseed

2 tablespoons unsalted butter

1 shallot, finely chopped

1 teaspoon minced fresh thyme

⅔ cup fruity, medium-bodied red wine, such as Pinot Noir, Côtes du Rhône, or Zinfandel

⅓ cup low-sodium chicken broth

1½ tablespoons minced fresh chives for garnish

QUALINESTI VEGETABLE STEW

In the world of Krynn, shortly after the ancient Kinslayer Wars, Prince Kith-Kanan appealed to his brother King Sithas for western sovereignty. His brother peacefully granted the western elves independence from the nation of Silvanesti. However, Kith-Kanan, the new king of the western elves, was met with decades of hardships resulting from the diaspora. Until their capital Qualinost was founded, his elven people struggled to find new ways of living off the land. Several simple and humble meals entered the repertoire of the elven diet, including "Harvest Prize," an artfully prepared baked vegetable casserole. Sourceable produce such as eggplant, zucchini, yellow squash, and tomato were thinly sliced then stacked in fanned layers upon fresh basil and tomato (crushed into a sauce), then drizzled with fresh and fragrant oils before roasting. This humble yet abundant dish could feed an entire elven village at little cost. Although the elves of Krynn now prepare variations of this dish year-round with inspired substitutions to harness the seasons, the combination below is the most classic and recommended.

Preheat the oven to 375°F with a rack in the middle of the oven.

In a 12-inch ovenproof skillet over medium heat, combine ¼ cup of the olive oil, half the garlic, and the thyme and cook, stirring, until fragrant and the garlic just begins to sizzle, 1 to 2 minutes. Scrape the mixture into a small bowl and set aside.

Add the remaining oil to the skillet over medium heat and allow the oil to warm until shimmering. Add the onion and ½ teaspoon salt and cook, stirring, until softened, about 4 minutes. Add the remaining garlic and cook, stirring, until fragrant, about 1 minute. Add the tomato puree, sugar, and pepper to taste. Bring to a simmer and cook, stirring occasionally, until slightly thickened, about 7 minutes. Adjust the seasoning with additional salt, if necessary, and set aside off the heat to cool slightly. Add 2 tablespoons of the basil and stir to mix; spread and smooth the mixture into an even layer in the skillet.

Working in concentric circles from the edges of the skillet toward the middle, neatly shingle the sliced zucchini, yellow squash, eggplant, and tomatoes, alternating and overlapping the vegetables and packing them tightly in a single layer. Drizzle the reserved garlic-thyme oil evenly over the vegetables and sprinkle with about ¾ teaspoon salt and ¾ teaspoon pepper. Cover the skillet and bake until the vegetables begin to soften, about 30 minutes. Remove the cover and continue baking until the vegetables are very tender and bubbling around the edges of the skillet, about 20 minutes more.

Rest the dish for 10 minutes, sprinkle with the remaining 2 tablespoons basil and serve.

SERVES 4

⅓ cup extra-virgin olive oil

5 garlic cloves, finely chopped

2 teaspoons minced fresh thyme

1 large yellow onion, finely chopped

Kosher salt

1 (15-ounce) can tomato puree

1 teaspoon sugar

Freshly ground black pepper

¼ cup chopped fresh basil

1 zucchini, sliced ¼ inch thick

1 yellow squash, sliced ¼ inch thick

1 Japanese or Chinese eggplant, sliced ¼ inch thick

4 plum tomatoes, sliced ¼ inch thick

COOK'S NOTE

Japanese and Chinese eggplants are long and slender, with a diameter similar to that of zucchini or the fat end of yellow squash. If you use globe eggplant instead, choose the skinniest one you can find and cut the slices to a similar size as the squashes and tomatoes. Make sure the curved side faces out when you arrange them in the skillet.

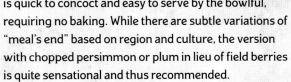

Meal's End

Heavy cream, foraged fruits, and a crushed dark meringue comprise a delightful combination of flavors that offer a light and colorful post-meal elven sweet. Elves aren't decadent and are resultantly not known for their culinary prowess with desserts, but this refreshing dish is quick to concoct and easy to serve by the bowlful, requiring no baking. While there are subtle variations of "meal's end" based on region and culture, the version with chopped persimmon or plum in lieu of field berries is quite sensational and thus recommended.

Coarsely chop 2 cups of the strawberries. In a bowl, mix the chopped strawberries with sugar to taste. Slice or quarter the remaining 1 cup berries. In a small bowl, mix these strawberries with sugar to taste.

With a stand mixer fitted with the whisk attachment, a handheld electric mixer, or a whisk, beat the cream until it is softly whipped, adding 1 tablespoon sugar once the cream has thickened. This will take 1 to 1½ minutes with a stand mixer on high speed. Fold in the yogurt and vanilla just until blended. Fold in the chopped berries and crumbled meringues.

Divide the mixture among four serving dishes, top with the sliced berries, and serve at once.

SERVES 4

3 cups fresh strawberries, rinsed and hulled (or a mix of berries)

Sugar as needed

1⅓ cups heavy cream

⅓ cup plain Greek yogurt (preferably whole milk) or crème fraîche

¼ teaspoon pure vanilla extract

2 ounces packaged or homemade cocoa or vanilla meringues, coarsely crumbled (about 1⅓ cups)

COOK'S NOTES

Serve the Meal's End immediately after making it because time is unkind to the texture of the meringues.

If you feel that your berries require a flavor boost, add about 1 tablespoon of pomegranate juice or berry liqueur, orange liqueur, port, or even cognac.

You can substitute blueberries, blackberries, or peeled and cubed persimmons for the 1 cup sliced or quartered strawberries.

The Inn of the Last Home

Main Road, Last Home (North) Solace

food

Daybreak meat platter . . . . .4 stl

Gully dwarf porridge with fruits & nuts . . .3 stl

Cornbread and butterwhip . . . . .1 stl

Beer bread (by the loaf) . . . . .2 stl

Flat bread with seasonal toppings . . . . .1 stl

Otik's Spiced Fried Potatoes* . . . . .3 stl

Meat stuffed mushrooms and cheese . . . . . . .2 stl

Daily dumplings (inquire) . . . . .3 stl

Dwarven Tide-me-overs* . . . . .3 stl

Stuffed Shirts (spinach pie) . . . . .3 stl

Green Onion Pancakes, fried with fresh cream . . 3 stl

Traveler's Stew with beef, carrot and onion* . . .3 stl

Venison & Bean Stew . . . . .4 stl

Rabbit, mustard-rubbed and long rice . . . . .5 stl

Pheasant with breads and wine gravy . . . . .6 stl

Shrimp (Tarsis style) . . . . .7 stl

Twice-fried sausages & twice-baked potatoes . . 5 stl

Tika's Stewed Woodchuck with seasonal roots . . 5 stl

Quince cheese hand pie . . . . .3 stl

Honeyed fig tarts . . . . .2 stl

Sour cream Walnut Cake by the slice . . . .2 stl

Dortberry pie by the slice . . . . .2 stl

Sliced fruits and fresh cream . . . . .1 stl

Kender kiffles . . . . .2 stl

Quith-pa table nosh* . . . . On the house
(as long as you're drinkin')

drinks

Irlymeyer's Dragonfire Punch (for the table) . . .2 stl

Ginger Root Tea . . . . .1 stl

Otik's Brandy . . . . .2 stl

Otik's Cider . . . . .2 stl

House Dark Ale . . . . .3 stl

House Light Ale . . . . .3 stl

Dwarven Mulled Wine* . . . . .4 stl

Par Salian's Tea* .3 stl

"Founded by Krale the Strong, this inn seated
atop one of Solace's great vallenwood trees
has been serving the finest foods in Ansalon
for generations. I, proprietor Otik Sandath,
proudly continue this tradition and welcome
you, stranger. Have a seat by the fire and try one
of our smooth ales or our spicy, fried potatoes,
made right here on the premises. And if you
need anything at all, Tika here can help."

3

DWARVEN CUISINE

Bangers and Smash • 89

Delzoun "Tide-Me-Overs" • 90

Underdark Lotus
with Fire Lichen Spread • 93

Miner's Pie • 95

Potato Leek Soup • 97

Smoked Sausages and Kraut
with Dwarven Mustard • 99

Corned Beef
and Cabbage • 100

Gully Dwarf
Homestyle Porridge • 101

Dwarven Flatbread • 103

Orange Mountain Duck • 104

Plate-of-Gold • 106

Black Pudding • 109

"'Yer pardon, fair lady,' the dwarf croaked, his voice cracking on every syllable. The woman twirled and looked at him curiously.

"'Might I be getting a bit o' food?' asked Bruenor, never one to mix up his priorities."

—R.A. SALVATORE, *THE HALFLING'S GEM*

Dwarves boast a surprisingly eclectic and adaptable palate for a traditionally sub-terranean folk, but there is one dietary constant regardless of location or culture: meat. Grains and vegetables complement hearty and practical family-style meals, usually featuring core proteins ranging from sheep and beef to pork and pheasant, with the occasional reptile, fungus, or oversize insect finding their way into the main courses of deeper-dwelling dwarves.

HARDY AND HEARTY

Standing roughly four feet tall with another foot of pride on top, dwarves were once primarily subterranean but have now increasingly populated surface coasts and plains, making cultural inroads into the villages and even cities of human-dominated worlds. An intensely private culture, these stout humanoids are hardworking and dedicated craftsmen—be it in mining, blacksmithing, weaponsmithing, stonework, or combat—and their prowess in the culinary arts is no exception. Dwarves are a stubborn, yet begrudgingly pliant breed, which has allowed their unique rituals, customs, and cuisine to endure regardless of the environment.

While dwarven dishes can sometimes taste one-note and homogenous to the uninitiated, their meals are surprisingly subtle to dwarven taste buds and can be a thoroughly well-rounded source of sustenance for various humanoids. However, few non-dwarves have ever tasted "true" dwarven cuisine, since most dwarven clans closely guard their secrets of the forge and the kitchen alike. Meanwhile, surface-dwelling dwarves are often savvy and resourceful, opting to incorporate locally sourced components—be it indigenous grains or the most readily available root vegetables—into their dishes in lieu of traditional ingredients. Nevertheless, their style of food remains constant, with savory and salty stews, marinated carved beasts, earthy root vegetables, and sauce-laden starches, all served in robust portions, dominating dwarven dinner tables alongside thick loaves of warm, dark bread for dipping and noshing. As for ales and mead, it's simply not a dwarven meal without them.

SALTY AND SOUR

Dwarves are a stubborn lot . . . and so are their palates. Nevertheless, they begrudgingly see the sense in accommodating a range of tastes, especially when traveling away from their mountain homes in the company of a multicultural band of adventurers. But in their native environments, dwarves of the mountains, and especially the hills (occasionally referred to as shield and gold dwarves, respectively), live in self-sustaining, clan-based societies that harvest and store great quantities of grain and dry-aged meats, planning carefully for the unforeseen. There is little room for waste or the superfluous in their culture or appetite. Regardless of what world they occupy, be it Krynn, Toril, Oerth, Eberron, or elsewhere, dwarves of the multiverse tend to exemplify constant attributes and even more steadfast tastes.

To that end, dwarven menus have evolved very little over the past millennia. Despite their well-documented obsession with all that shines, heritage is the one thing a dwarf values above any sum of mithral or precious gems and they do so with an almost hubristic commitment. Holidays and traditions such as Midwinter and Feast of the Moon remain dear to modern dwarves, and with them the requisite ceremonial dishes. Traveling dwarves are open to other types of food, (and they will never say no to a homemade meal), but they will proudly let you know how a dwarven touch, inevitably a savory one, might have improved it. More often than not, this just means taking a recipe and doubling the meat.

Pragmatic to the core, dwarves enjoy food and appreciate the ritual of a shared meal, but they do not belabor over its importance or the small talk that goes with it, preferring to eat and get on with it. They love to feast, but reserve communal dining for celebrations; the everyday meal of a dwarf is consumed hastily while on the job. Wholesome, often one-course meals provide essential nourishment and brief repose for these unflinchingly hardworking beings, and such meals are packed and eaten with little ceremony. When dwarves do eat together, storytelling and seemingly never-ending songs often intersect with mealtime, providing a vital chance for elders to dispense lessons and learnings when a clan is gathered beside a great hearth at the same table. It is on such occasions that the fruits of dwarven mining and craftsmanship are on display in their elaborate engraved flatware made from the most precious metals, and the enormous clanking steins bristling with gems.

Dwarves of the Underdark, commonly known as gray dwarves or duergar, have developed a fungi-based diet, since livestock and most vegetables are scantly available, let alone sustainable, below the surface. Duergar forage accordingly and have developed a nuanced tongue for fungal variances, and cleverly season the "meat" to stimulate, rather than modify, its natural flavors, favoring acidic, spicy, and briny flavors to salty or savory, based on the local availability of ingredients. They have a penchant for nurturing great fields of diverse mycological vegetation, complemented with tubers or roots.

The other primary difference between surface-dwelling dwarves and duergar is the level of alcohol consumption. Hill and mountain dwarves have a legendary appetite for beer and ale, one so profound that it might be said that the food that accompanies them is an afterthought. Duergar appreciate the occasional drink but are not a celebratory lot. They imbibe in solemnity and considerable moderation. While duergar maintain their cousins' utilitarian ideals of harvesting and stockpiling basic available edibles, their distant kin, gully dwarves, have taken orthodox dwarven pragmatism to the next extreme, foregoing harvesting all together and scavenging without qualm.

SECRET SPICES
A dwarven cupboard is often simple, well-organized, and deeply stocked. It's uncommon to see rare spices in the kitchen, with flavor additives erring on the tried and true. A common misconception about dwarves is that they lack adventurous culinary spirit or imagination, but in fact they have highly sensitive taste buds, often overwhelmed by bright, piquant, or saccharine flavors. They prefer their soups dense, their sauces thick, their meats long-aged or marinated over days, their vegetables roasted or sautéed (rarely raw), with salads and pescatarian options uncommon (save for duergar), though dried fruits and salted legumes might find their way into trail mix or iron rations. Although dwarves crave and utilize an immensely broad base of staples, key culinary decisions are often made by first choosing a stout and then selecting a main course to pair with it. And the dwarves' knack for a good liquor-meat pairing is usually on point, with their choice of drink serving to activate new flavors in the dish or, at minimum, enhance the inherent.

Bangers and Smash

Nothing makes a dwarf stand quite so tall in the morning as a breakfast platter steaming with sausages and smashed baby potatoes. These traditional sausages are sheet pan–baked with succulent tomatoes that soak up the juices and practically *polymorph* into a meat themselves. Dwarven smiths are known to keep their bangers and smash warm all morning in an iron skillet that rests atop their furnace, so they can plunge a fork into it and satisfy their appetites without straying too far from their duties.

Preheat the oven to 450°F with a rack in the middle of the oven.

On a large rimmed baking sheet, roast the potatoes until very tender, about 40 minutes.

Remove the baking sheet from the oven (leave the oven on) and set aside to cool, about 10 minutes. Transfer the potatoes to a bowl, brush the baking sheet with 2 tablespoons of the olive oil, and sprinkle the sheet lightly with salt and pepper. Return the potatoes to the baking sheet, spacing them about 2 inches apart. With the bottom of a mug or another baking sheet (to do all the potatoes at once), sharply press down on the potatoes to break their skins and compress the flesh to a thickness of about 1 inch (do not smash them thinner). Brush the potatoes with 2 tablespoons olive oil, return them to the oven, and continue to roast for 15 minutes. Remove the baking sheet from the oven, turn the potatoes over, and rearrange them over about half the baking sheet.

In the now-empty bowl, toss the leeks with 3 tablespoons olive oil, season with salt and pepper, and spread them on the empty side of the baking sheet. Add the sausages to the now-empty bowl, add 1½ teaspoons olive oil, and toss to coat. Arrange the sausages over the leeks.

Roast for 8 minutes. Remove the baking sheet from the oven, move the sausages to the side, stir the leeks, spread them over about two-thirds of the empty space on the baking sheet, and replace the sausages over the leeks.

In the now-empty bowl, toss the tomatoes with the remaining 1½ teaspoons oil to coat. Sprinkle lightly with salt and pepper and toss again. Spread the tomatoes in the empty space on the baking sheet and continue to roast until the skins burst, the sausages are warmed through, and the potatoes are crisp, about 10 minutes more.

Transfer the potatoes, tomatoes, sausages, and leeks to a serving platter, sprinkle with the parsley, and serve.

SERVES 4

1½ pounds (about 16) small red-skinned or Yukon gold creamer potatoes, scrubbed

½ cup extra-virgin olive oil

Kosher salt and freshly ground black pepper

2 leeks, white and light green parts, halved lengthwise and cut into 1-inch pieces

4 to 8 fresh or fully cooked chicken or pork sausages (breakfast sausages or any flavor of your choice)

1 pound large cherry tomatoes

2 tablespoons chopped fresh parsley

Delzoun "Tide-Me-Overs"

Beef, pork, onions, and a smattering of dwarven seasoning are all rolled up into delicious little balls that are ideal for snacking or as a main banquet course. These "meatballs," as they are known to many in the multiverse, are sometimes served with a side of freshly crushed tart berries for dwarves on the go, but they are best when drenched in a sweet, dark dwarven gravy made with chicken broth and enlivened with brown sugar, lemon, and soy sauce. While these are customary consumables at Hornmoot, the traditional human-dwarven trading festival that marks the dawn of Spring, there isn't a holiday on the eventful dwarven calendar that doesn't feature these scrumptious meats on the menu.

SERVES 4

¼ cup heavy cream

1 egg

2 slices dark bread (such as rye), crusts discarded, remainder torn into pieces

3 tablespoons unsalted butter

1 small yellow onion, finely chopped

Kosher salt

¼ teaspoon ground allspice

8 ounces ground pork

8 ounces lean ground beef

1 teaspoon baking powder

Freshly ground black pepper

2 tablespoons all-purpose flour

1⅓ cups low-sodium chicken broth

1 teaspoon light brown sugar

1½ teaspoons soy sauce

½ teaspoon fresh lemon juice

3 tablespoons finely chopped fresh dill or parsley

In a large bowl, whisk together the cream and egg. Add the bread, mix well, and set aside, stirring occasionally, until the bread is softened, about 20 minutes. Using a fork or a sturdy spoon, mash the bread to a paste and set aside.

Meanwhile, in a skillet over medium heat, melt 1 tablespoon of the butter. Add the onion and ½ teaspoon salt and cook, stirring, until softened, about 4 minutes. Add the allspice and cook, stirring, until fragrant, about 40 seconds. Remove from the heat and let cool to room temperature.

Preheat the oven to 475°F with a rack in the middle of the oven. Coat a large wire rack with nonstick cooking spray and set it in a large rimmed baking sheet.

Add the cooled onion mixture, pork, ground beef, baking powder, 1 teaspoon salt, and ½ teaspoon pepper to the bread paste and, using a large spoon or your hands, mix until well combined and uniform.

With moistened hands, form the mixture into generous 1-tablespoon-size balls. Arrange the meatballs on the rack in the baking sheet and bake until lightly browned, about 20 minutes, rotating the pan halfway through.

Wipe out the skillet used for the onions to remove any stray onion bits, set it over medium heat, and melt the remaining 2 tablespoons butter. Stirring constantly, cook until fragrant and a shade darker, 1 to 2 minutes. Add the flour and cook, stirring constantly, until golden,

CONTINUED ON PAGE 92 →

DELZOUN "TIDE-ME-OVERS,"
CONTINUED

===< COOK'S NOTE >===

The sauce will thicken quickly as it cools. You can loosen the consistency by whisking in extra chicken broth or water, about 1 tablespoon at a time, until you have achieved the desired texture.

2 to 3 minutes. Switch to a whisk and, whisking constantly, gradually add the broth. Continuing to whisk often, cook for about 2 minutes. Add the brown sugar, soy sauce, lemon juice, and ¼ teaspoon pepper and continue to whisk and cook until thickened, about 2 minutes more.

Add the meatballs to the sauce and simmer, stirring occasionally, until heated through, about 4 minutes. Stir in most of the dill and taste and adjust the seasoning with additional salt and pepper, if necessary. Transfer to a serving dish, sprinkle with the remaining dill, and serve hot.

Underdark Lotus with Fire Lichen Spread

Sometimes called "fungus two ways," this zesty duergar essential is sure to rouse the taste buds of even the most spice-crazed tiefling. Made from the bright-white roots of Underdark lotus or bluecap fungus, these tubers are steamed and then cut thin into crunchy, round slices, perfect for dipping. However, if you can't source authentic Underdark produce, sliced radishes have a similar texture and flavor, and even jicama, cucumbers, or romaine lettuce can work in a pinch. The star of the show, however, is the spread, made from the pale-orange fire lichen fungus that is ground into a delectable spicy paste. But make sure to keep a waterorb handy—this stuff is hot!

Preheat the oven to 425°F with a rack in the middle of the oven.

On a large rimmed baking sheet, toss together the chickpeas, carrots, cumin, cayenne, and 2 tablespoons of the olive oil. Sprinkle with ½ teaspoon salt and lots of pepper. Roast until the carrots are tender, about 25 minutes.

Transfer the roasted carrots and chickpeas to a food processor or blender. Add the water, lemon juice, tahini, and remaining 1 tablespoon olive oil. Blend until completely smooth, adding more water, 1 tablespoon at a time, as needed to make the spread smooth and creamy.

Spoon the spread into a serving bowl, set the bowl on a large plate, and drizzle with olive oil. Arrange the radishes, sliced cucumbers, or romaine around the bowl, ready for dipping, and serve immediately.

COOK'S NOTES

To create the lotus shape, arrange the vegetables around the bowl of spread as if they were the petals of a flower.

You can use your favorite kind of vegetable for dipping.

SERVES 6

1 (15-ounce) can chickpeas, drained and rinsed

1 pound carrots (about 4 large), peeled and chopped

¾ teaspoon cumin seeds or sweet paprika

1 teaspoon cayenne

3 tablespoons olive oil, plus more for drizzling

Kosher salt and freshly ground black pepper

⅔ cup cold water, plus more as needed

¼ cup fresh lemon juice

¼ cup tahini

Radishes, sliced cucumbers, or romaine lettuce leaves for dipping

Miner's Pie

The Miner's Pie, sometimes referred to as a "shepherd's pie" by humans and halflings, is a truly hearty one-stop meal for the tireless dwarf in all of us. Ground beef (or lamb or venison), sweet corn, peas, onions, and leeks are crusted by a potato mash topped with cheese. This is one of the few dwarven dishes readily served at inns across Faerûn, particularly those of the North and Heartlands, likely because the human variant borrows much from this dwarven classic.

MAKE THE FILLING. In a very large skillet over medium-high heat, warm the olive oil until shimmering. Add the onion, leek, bay leaf, and ½ teaspoon salt and cook, stirring frequently, until softened, about 4 minutes. Add the ground beef and cook, stirring and breaking up any clumps, until no longer pink, about 10 minutes. Add the garlic, thyme, and tomato paste and cook, stirring constantly, until fragrant, about 1 minute. Adjust the heat to medium, add the flour, and cook, stirring constantly, for 1 to 2 minutes, until the flour is completely blended in. Add the ale, broth, and ¾ teaspoon salt. Adjust the heat to high and bring to a simmer, using a wooden spoon to scrape the bottom of the skillet to loosen and dissolve any browned bits stuck to the pan, about 1 minute. Adjust the heat to medium-low and cook, stirring and scraping the bottom of the skillet occasionally, until the filling is thickened but still saucy, about 15 minutes.

Add the corn and peas and set the skillet aside, off the heat to cool slightly. Remove the bay leaf, add most of the parsley, and stir to mix. Taste and adjust the seasoning with additional salt, if necessary, and pepper to taste. Scrape the mixture into a broiler-safe 2-quart casserole dish, spread evenly, and set aside.

Preheat the oven to 450°F with a rack in the upper-middle of the oven.

CONTINUED ON PAGE 96 →

SERVES 4 TO 6

FILLING

1½ tablespoons olive oil

1 yellow onion, chopped

1 large leek, white and light green parts, halved lengthwise and cut into ¾-inch pieces

1 bay leaf

Kosher salt

2 pounds ground beef

3 garlic cloves, finely chopped

2 teaspoons finely chopped fresh thyme

4 tablespoons tomato paste

3 tablespoons all-purpose flour

½ cup ale, such as IPA

1 cup low-sodium chicken broth

¾ cup frozen corn, thawed

¾ cup frozen peas, thawed

¼ cup chopped fresh parsley

Freshly ground black pepper

INGREDIENTS CONTINUED →

MINER'S PIE,

CONTINUED

TOPPING

3 pounds russet potatoes, peeled,
cut into 1-inch chunks, and rinsed well

3 tablespoons unsalted butter, melted

⅔ cup whole milk or half-and-half

Kosher salt and freshly ground
black pepper

⅓ cup freshly grated Parmesan cheese

2 eggs, beaten

¾ cup coarsely grated Monterey Jack
or Colby cheese

MEANWHILE, MAKE THE TOPPING. Put the potatoes in a steaming basket. Fill a Dutch oven or large saucepan with enough water to just reach the bottom of the steaming basket and bring to a boil over high heat. Set the steamer basket in the pot, cover, adjust the heat to medium-high, and cook until the potatoes are very tender, about 20 minutes. Remove the steamer basket and pour the water out of the pot.

Set a potato ricer over the pot and rice the potatoes into it. Add the melted butter and stir it into the potatoes. Add the milk, 1½ teaspoons salt, pepper to taste, and the Parmesan and stir to incorporate. Taste and adjust the seasoning with additional salt and pepper, if necessary, and set aside to cool for about 20 minutes.

Add the eggs to the potatoes and stir to incorporate. Spoon the potatoes over the filling, spreading them evenly and making sure they reach to the edges of the casserole dish. Sprinkle evenly with the Monterey Jack. Place the dish on a large baking sheet and bake until the filling is heated through and the potatoes are puffed slightly, about 20 minutes.

Turn on the broiler and cook until the top is golden brown, 5 to 7 minutes. Sprinkle with the remaining parsley and serve hot.

Potato Leek Soup

A Mithral Hall mainstay of Faerûn, dwarven potato leek soup is a stalwart starter that is prepared as thick as mortals can stand it. Served year-round, this dense and nutritious vegetable blend is perfect for warming the limbs and souls of dwarves subjected to the unrelenting cold of damp subterranean life.

Sloppily ladled into oversize ramekins and prepared voluminously in full anticipation of seconds (and thirds), it's made to satiate the bottomless hunger of weary warriors or tireless miners. You can't go wrong with toppings such as chopped scallions, chives, and bacon!

In a large heavy pot over medium heat, fry the bacon, turning it over as necessary, until well-rendered and lightly browned, about 13 minutes. Use a slotted spoon or tongs to transfer the bacon to a paper towel.

Add the leeks, celery, and thyme to the pot and cook, stirring, until the vegetables soften, about 5 minutes. Add the potatoes, broth, and 1 teaspoon salt. Simmer until the potatoes are soft, 15 to 20 minutes.

Remove the soup from the heat. Using an immersion blender, blend until smooth. Alternatively, blend the soup in batches using a countertop blender.

Return the soup to the pot over medium heat. Stir in the cream and simmer until slightly thickened, about 5 minutes. Taste and season with black pepper and more salt, if needed. Crumble the cooked bacon. Serve each bowl of soup piping hot and topped with bacon (alternatively, the soup can be served cold).

SERVES 6

2 slices thick-cut bacon

3 leeks, white and light green parts, thinly sliced

3 celery stalks, chopped

2 teaspoons fresh thyme leaves

2 pounds russet potatoes, peeled and cut into 1-inch pieces

4 cups low-sodium chicken broth

Kosher salt

1 cup heavy cream

Freshly ground black pepper

Smoked Sausages and Kraut with Dwarven Mustard

At the end of a long day working in fiery forges and lava-filled mines, most dwarves have an insatiable craving for salty and sour foods, always paired with a strong ale. Nothing hits the spot quite like a heaping plate of dwarven smoked sausages with mounds of briny sauerkraut—a recipe, according to legend, forged and handed down by the Dwarffather god Moradin himself! When possible, serve these plump sausages with dwarven mustard, a lightly spiced, sweet, stone-ground condiment. In some regions of Cormyr, this mustard is widely regarded as a cure-all.

In a large pot over medium-low heat, warm the vegetable oil. Add the onion and cook, stirring occasionally, until completely soft and starting to caramelize, about 15 minutes. Add the apple, sugar, juniper berries (if using), sauerkraut, water, ½ teaspoon salt, and several grinds of pepper. Cover the pot and cook until the apple is soft, 25 to 35 minutes.

Meanwhile, bring the beer to a simmer in a wide saucepan. Poke the sausages in several places with a fork. Add them to the pan with the beer and cook until warmed through, 5 to 10 minutes.

In a small bowl, stir together the mustard and sour cream.

Spoon some of the sauerkraut mixture onto each serving plate. Use tongs to place a sausage on top. If you'd like the sauerkraut to be a little saucier, spoon 1 to 2 tablespoons of the warm beer over the top. Serve with the mustard mixture on the side.

SERVES 6

3 tablespoons vegetable oil

1 yellow onion, finely chopped

1 large apple, peeled, cored, and cut into ½-inch pieces

1 teaspoon sugar

1 teaspoon juniper berries (optional)

4 cups sauerkraut, drained, rinsed, and squeezed dry

Kosher salt and freshly ground black pepper

1½ cups water

2 cups dark beer

6 smoked sausages, such as kielbasa or bratwurst

½ cup stone-ground mustard

¼ cup sour cream

Corned Beef and Cabbage

From the mines of the Ironroot Mountains to the halls of the Iron Hills, this savory winter repast is a favorite of dwarves everywhere. Hungry miners will blush pinker than the beef itself when their noses catch the distinct scent of coriander, allspice, peppercorns, bay leaves, thyme, and red pepper flakes wafting from a full-to-the-brim cauldron. Served in a light, tangy broth with generous helpings of boiled cabbage and doused in vinegar, this dish is sure to satisfy the salt cravings of even the saltiest dwarves (just as long as you don't forget the ale).

SERVES 4

4 garlic cloves, smashed and peeled

3 tablespoons store-bought mixed pickling spice

1 (3-pound) corned beef brisket, flat (or thin) cut, rinsed well and fat trimmed to about a ¼-inch-thick layer, if necessary

1 yellow onion, quartered

2 carrots, peeled and chopped

2 celery ribs, trimmed and chopped

2 cups low-sodium chicken broth

1½ pounds (about 16) small red-skinned or Yukon gold creamer potatoes, scrubbed

1 (2-pound) small head green cabbage, tough outer leaves removed, cut through the core into 6 wedges

Kosher salt and freshly ground black pepper

3 tablespoons unsalted butter, softened and cut into small pieces

3 tablespoons chopped fresh parsley

White wine vinegar for serving (optional)

COOK'S NOTE

When shopping for corned beef (or brisket, from which corned beef is made), you'll commonly see two cuts—flat (sometimes called thin) and point. Flat-cut is more uniformly shaped and thus will cook more evenly.

Preheat the oven to 300°F with a rack in the middle position of the oven.

In a large Dutch oven, combine the garlic, pickling spice, corned beef, onion, carrots, and celery. Add the broth and enough water to just cover the meat and cook, covered, until the corned beef is super-tender (a paring knife should slip easily into the meat), about 4 hours. Transfer the meat to a baking dish; trim and discard the fat, if desired. Strain and reserve the cooking liquid, and discard the solids. Pour about 1 cup of the liquid over the meat, cover the dish tightly with foil, and let rest for about 30 minutes.

Pour the strained cooking liquid into a fat separator or measuring cup and rest until the fat rises to the surface, about 10 minutes. If you are using a fat separator, pour the liquid into another container; if you are using a measuring cup, tilt it and use a wide, shallow soup spoon to skim any fat off the surface and discard it.

Return the liquid to the Dutch oven, add the potatoes, set the pot over medium-high heat, and bring to a simmer. Adjust the heat to medium-low, cover, and simmer until the potatoes just begin to soften, about 8 minutes. Add the cabbage, submerge it in the liquid as best you can (arrange the potatoes among the cabbage wedges), replace the cover, adjust the heat to medium-high, and return to a simmer. Adjust the heat to medium-low and simmer until the potatoes and cabbage are both tender, 10 to 14 minutes more, turning over the cabbage wedges after 6 minutes.

Meanwhile, place the meat on a cutting board, slice it against the grain into thin slices, and set the slices on a large serving platter. Using a slotted spoon, transfer the vegetables to a large bowl and sprinkle them with salt, if necessary, and pepper to taste. Scatter the butter pieces over the vegetables, wait a moment for the butter to begin to melt, and gently turn over the vegetables to distribute the butter. Arrange the potatoes and cabbage around the meat on the platter, sprinkle the parsley over the meat and vegetables, and serve with vinegar on the side, if desired.

Gully Dwarf Homestyle Porridge

If you've ever attended a gully dwarf meal, you've probably only done so once. As scavengers who dwell in the deepest, darkest, and dirtiest parts of subterranean spaces, their dining habits are not exactly refined. But a wholesale dismissal of their cuisine would be throwing out the baby with the bathwater (which gully dwarves are known to drink on occasion). Traditional gully dwarf porridge calls for a grainy stew chock-full of . . . you don't want to know. However, their more civilized dwarven cousins have developed their own morningfeast dish, which cleverly pokes fun at the inedible original. Their version, also called "dirty porridge," comprises of a creamy oatmeal-style base chock-full of dates, chopped nuts, dark sugars, and a dose of cream. Dwarves have even been known to brew a savory "gully dwarf porridge" containing leftover sausage bits, streaks of bacon fat, and finely chopped scallions in a grits-style "broth." Regardless of which version you eat, this porridge from the world of Krynn is a true random encounter for your taste buds.

In a large saucepan over medium heat, melt the butter. Add the oats and cook, stirring constantly, until they smell fragrant, nutty, and toasty and look a shade darker, about 4 minutes.

Add the water, adjust the heat to medium-high, and bring to a simmer, stirring constantly. Add the milk, adjust the heat to medium-low and simmer gently, stirring occasionally, until the mixture is thickened to the consistency of applesauce and the oats are tender but chewy, 10 to 15 minutes. Add the salt and 3 tablespoons brown sugar and stir to incorporate.

Remove the pan from the heat, cover, and let rest for about 5 minutes; the oatmeal will thicken to about the consistency of pudding. Serve at once, topping each serving evenly with about 1½ teaspoons cream and 1 teaspoon brown sugar.

COOK'S NOTES

Cooking oats in a mixture of water and milk provides a good balance of richness (using all milk can make the porridge overly rich, especially once the cream garnish is added).

Add the water to the toasted oats before the milk, otherwise it might foam up.

The oatmeal will continue to thicken as it cools, so make sure to serve it hot.

SERVES 4

1½ tablespoons unsalted butter

1 cup steel-cut oats

3¼ cups water

½ cup low-fat or whole milk

¼ teaspoon kosher salt

3 tablespoons light brown sugar, plus 4 teaspoons for garnish

2 tablespoons heavy cream or half-and-half for garnish

> *"Six gully dwarves trailed after them, carrying heavy pots of what smelled like oatmeal"*
>
> **—MARGARET WEIS AND TRACY HICKMAN,** *DRAGONS OF AUTUMN TWILIGHT*

Dwarven Flatbread

Generations of dwarven smiths have relied on this toothsome snack bread to get them through long, arduous workdays, and to their next meal. According to folklore, these tasty flat loaves weren't created in the kitchen, but rather at the forge as ever-industrious, hungry dwarven craftsman utilized the only materials they had available: flour, oil, water, salt, a hearth, and a hammer. The result? Flat bread. Sometimes served pan-griddled, other times fried, this bread can be eaten plain, topped with cheese or duergar fire lichen spread (see page 93), or used to soak up all of those savory juices and sauces from what dwarven diners showed up for in the first place—meat!

In a large bowl, whisk together the flour, baking powder, baking soda, salt, and herb blend to combine. Make a well in the center, add the olive oil and yogurt. With a wooden spoon or your hands, stir around the perimeter of the well to incorporate the wet and dry ingredients; the mixture will look a little rough and shaggy.

Lightly flour a work surface, scoop the dough onto it, and knead until the dough is smooth and uniform, adding a tiny amount of flour as you go if the dough becomes too sticky. Divide the dough into eight equal portions, gently roll each portion into a ball, cover with a clean kitchen towel, and let rest for 15 minutes.

Preheat the oven to 200°F (or the lowest temperature possible) with a rack in the middle of the oven.

With a rolling pin, roll one of the dough balls into a circle about 7 inches in diameter and ¼ inch thick. In a 10-inch heavy skillet (preferably cast iron) over medium heat, warm 1½ teaspoons of the vegetable oil until shimmering. Tilt the skillet to coat the entire cooking surface with oil, carefully place the dough circle in the skillet, and cook, undisturbed, until spotty brown on the bottom and slightly puffed, 3 to 4 minutes. Turn the bread over and continue to cook, undisturbed, until the second side is spotty brown as well, 3 to 4 minutes more. Transfer the bread to a baking sheet or ovenproof plate and place it in the oven to stay warm. Working with one dough ball and 1½ teaspoons oil at a time, repeat to roll, cook, and keep the remaining rounds warm. Note that as the pan accumulates and retains heat from previous batches, the cooking time may decrease by up to a minute. Serve warm and fresh.

SERVES 4

1½ cups all-purpose flour, plus more for dusting

1½ teaspoons baking powder

½ teaspoon baking soda

1½ teaspoons kosher salt

2½ teaspoons dried herb blend (such as Italian seasoning, herbes de Provence, or za'atar), crushed

3 tablespoons extra-virgin olive oil

⅔ cup plain low-fat Greek yogurt or whole milk

¼ cup neutral-tasting oil, such as vegetable, canola, safflower, or grapeseed

COOK'S NOTE

Skillet breads are a great canvas for customizing with simple toppings, such as finely chopped roasted red pepper or caramelized onions, or a schmear of ricotta cheese, added just before serving.

Orange Mountain Duck

Dwarves are widely renowned for their "unsweet tooth," but that doesn't deny them good taste, as evidenced by the southern Faerûnian gold dwarves' affinity for orange and persimmon mountain duck. The uniquely hot-and-tart sauce brightens the succulent gamey meat and yields a divine duck-skin treat. Perhaps years of living near humans wore them down or broadened their palate, but it is said modern dwarves have actually come to blows over the coveted crispy skin alone! While this dish might not grace the subterranean banquet halls of days long gone, it is surely on the surface dwarf menus of today.

SERVES 4

3 or 4 oranges, preferably navels

4 boneless duck breast halves (about 8 ounces each)

Kosher salt and freshly ground black pepper

1 shallot, minced

1 teaspoon minced fresh thyme

½ cup low-sodium chicken broth

1½ tablespoons honey

1½ tablespoons brandy or cognac

Pinch of cayenne

1 tablespoon unsalted butter

2 tablespoons chopped fresh parsley

1 firm-ripe Fuyu persimmon, peeled and diced into neat ¼-inch pieces (optional)

Finely grate 2 teaspoons zest from one of the oranges and set aside. Cut the peel and pith off the zested and a second orange. Working over a strainer set in a bowl, separate the orange segments. Discard any seeds and reserve the segments. Shake the strainer so all the juice drips into the bowl; pour the juice into a measuring cup. If necessary, squeeze one or both of the remaining oranges for enough juice to equal ⅔ cup and then set aside.

Preheat the oven to 200°F with the rack in the middle of the oven. With a sharp paring knife, cut four or five diagonal slashes in the skin on each duck breast half, taking care to cut down to, but not into, the flesh. Dry the halves well and sprinkle all over with salt and pepper.

Place the duck breasts skin-side down in a large nonstick skillet, set the skillet over medium heat, and cook, undisturbed, until most of the fat is rendered (if necessary, pour or spoon the fat out of the skillet occasionally) and the skin is deeply browned and crisp, 12 to 14 minutes, adjusting the heat, if necessary, to prevent scorching. Turn the halves skin-side up and continue cooking, undisturbed, until an instant-read thermometer in the thickest part registers about 125°F for medium-rare or 130° to 135°F for medium, 2 to 8 minutes more. Transfer the duck to a heatproof plate, tent loosely with foil, and place it in the oven to rest and keep warm, about 5 minutes.

Pour or spoon off all but 1 tablespoon of the fat from the skillet. Return the skillet to medium-low heat, add the shallot, thyme, and ½ teaspoon salt and cook, stirring, until softened, about 1 minute. Add the orange juice, adjust the heat to medium-high, and bring to a simmer. Simmer, stirring occasionally, until the consistency is slightly syrupy and the juice is reduced by half, about 4 minutes.

Add the broth and any accumulated duck juices to the skillet, return to a simmer, and simmer vigorously, stirring occasionally, until the consistency is slightly syrupy and the volume is reduced by half, 3 to 4 minutes more. Adjust the heat to medium-low and add the honey, brandy, cayenne, and reserved orange zest. Simmer, stirring, to melt and incorporate the honey and brandy, about 1 minute more. Add the butter and stir constantly while it melts and incorporates into the sauce. Taste and adjust the seasoning with additional salt and pepper, if necessary. Add most of the parsley and stir to incorporate. Pour or spoon about half of the sauce onto a warm serving plate.

Meanwhile, diagonally cut each duck breast half into ½-inch slices. Fan the slices over the sauce, top with the reserved orange segments, persimmon (if using), and the remaining sauce. Sprinkle with the remaining parsley and serve hot.

PLATE-OF-GOLD

Dwarves aren't known for eating their vegetables, but when the vegetables are drenched in a salty, golden batter and oil-fried until crisp, they can't get enough of them! Don't forget to finish these fried delights with a dousing of "golden sauce"—a syrupy, sweet confection laced with a citrus accent. This dish is particularly popular among surface dwarves who have greater access to fresh produce and root vegetables.

SERVES 4 AS AN APPETIZER

SWEET AND SOUR SAUCE

⅓ cup apricot or peach jam
or orange marmalade

⅓ cup ketchup

3 tablespoons cider vinegar

1 tablespoon light or dark
brown sugar

2 teaspoons soy sauce

½ teaspoon chile-garlic sauce
(optional)

Kosher salt

TEMPURA

About 1½ quarts canola or other
high-smoke-point oil for frying

⅔ cup cake flour

3 tablespoons all-purpose flour

Kosher salt

⅔ cup plus 1 tablespoon sparkling
water, cold

8 ounces fresh shiitake mushrooms,
stemmed, very large caps halved, cold

1 sweet potato, peeled, halved
lengthwise, and cut crosswise into
¼-inch slices, cold

1 yellow onion, trimmed, halved pole
to pole, and cut lengthwise into ½-inch
slivers, cold

MAKE THE SAUCE. In a small saucepan over medium heat, warm the jam, stirring, until mostly fluid, 3 to 5 minutes. Add the ketchup, vinegar, brown sugar, soy sauce, chile-garlic sauce (if using), and ½ teaspoon salt and whisk to combine. Bring to a simmer and cook, whisking, to blend the flavors, about 1 minute. Set aside to cool to room temperature. Taste and adjust the seasoning with additional salt, if necessary.

MAKE THE TEMPURA. Line a large, rimmed baking sheet with a double layer of paper towels and set aside. Clip a deep-fry or candy thermometer to the side of a heavy 5-quart Dutch oven, add the oil, and warm over medium-high heat to 390°F. Preheat the oven to 200°F. Place a wire rack on a second large, rimmed baking sheet and set aside.

Meanwhile, fill a large bowl about one-third full with ice and about 1½ cups water. In a medium (preferably stainless-steel) bowl that will fit in the larger bowl, whisk together the cake and all-purpose flours and ¾ teaspoon salt; set this bowl in the bowl with the ice water to chill the flour mixture. When the oil reaches 390°F, add the sparkling water to the flour mixture and stir just until the wet and dry are incorporated, but still a little lumpy; do not overmix.

Working with about eight pieces at a time, use tongs or chopsticks to dip them in the batter to coat thoroughly. Allow any excess batter to drip off, then slip them into the oil and fry until slightly puffed and pale gold, adjusting the heat as necessary to maintain 390°F, stirring to prevent sticking, and turning the pieces over in the oil once or twice to promote even frying, 5 to 6 minutes for each batch. With a spider skimmer, slotted spoon, or long tongs, transfer the tempura to the paper towel–lined baking sheet to drain for about 30 seconds. Sprinkle lightly with salt and place on the wire rack set on the baking sheet and put in the oven to keep warm. Allow the oil to recover to 390°F and fry the remaining batches. Serve with the sweet and sour sauce.

Black Pudding

No, not that black pudding! Eating real monsters is precarious play. Sure, some are considered delicacies and host to exquisite flavors of unimaginable complexity, but most are full of toxins and poisons that simply aren't worth the risk, to say nothing of what it takes to actually capture and kill your dinner. Inspired by one of those nasty dungeon-dwelling beasties and based on a goblin dish called "elf pudding" (you don't want to know), this traditional coffee and chocolate mousse is sure to satisfy even the most discerning dwarven palate. This dense caffeinated dessert is known to keep dwarves working their forges until the wee hours. Eat it before it eats you!

In a heavy saucepan, whisk together the brown sugar, espresso powder, cocoa powder, cornstarch, and salt, breaking up any brown sugar lumps as you go. Add the egg yolks and cream and whisk, reaching into the corners of the pan, until the mixture is smooth and uniform. Add the milk and whisk until incorporated.

Set the pan over medium heat and cook, whisking constantly and reaching into the corners of the pan, until the mixture is thickened and bubbling across its surface, 8 to 10 minutes. Continue cooking for about 1 minute more. Remove from the heat; add the butter, vanilla, coffee liqueur, and brandy; and whisk to melt and incorporate the butter fully.

Set a fine-mesh strainer over a bowl. Pour in the pudding and, with a flexible spatula, fold and stir the pudding gently to work it through the strainer. With a piece of parchment paper or plastic wrap, cover the pudding, pressing the paper or wrap directly onto the pudding surface.

Refrigerate until cold and set, at least 4 or up to 12 hours. At serving time, stir the pudding gently until smooth and then top with chocolate shavings and whipped cream, if using.

SERVES 4

⅔ cup packed light brown sugar

¼ cup instant espresso powder

3 tablespoons Dutch-processed cocoa powder

3 tablespoons cornstarch

½ teaspoon kosher salt

3 egg yolks

¾ cup heavy cream

2¾ cups whole milk

¼ cup unsalted butter

1½ teaspoons pure vanilla extract

1 tablespoon coffee liqueur, such as Kahlua

2 teaspoons brandy or cognac

Chocolate shavings for serving

Very lightly sweetened whipped cream for serving (optional)

COOK'S NOTE

Avoid substituting the Dutch-processed cocoa powder here, because it's darker than natural cocoa and has a distinct flavor. You will be able to taste the cocoa in the pudding, but the espresso will be the dominant flavor.

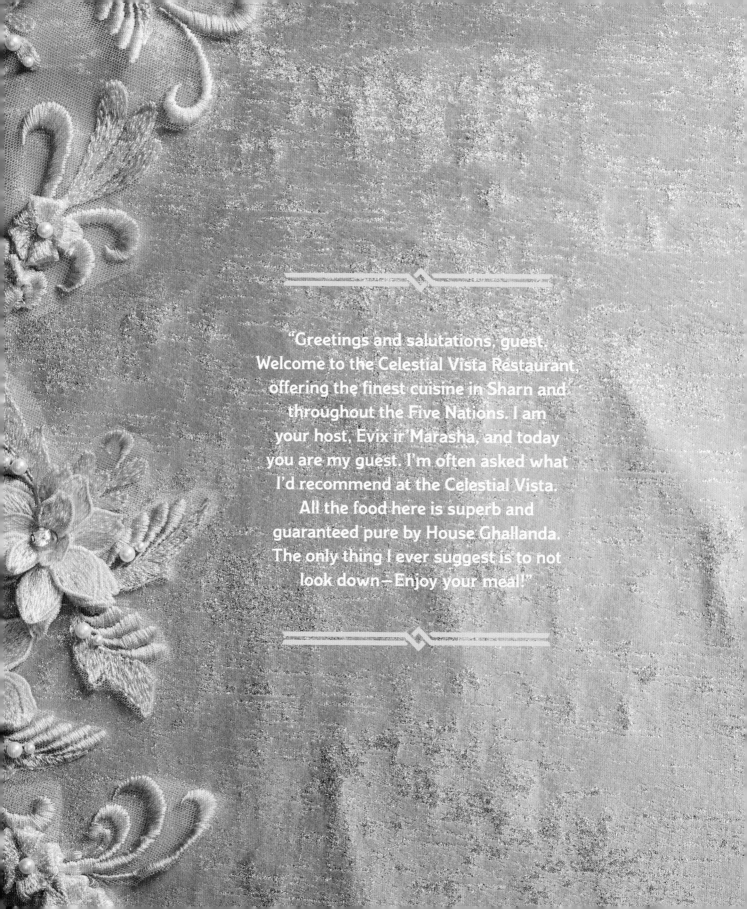

"Greetings and salutations, guest.
Welcome to the Celestial Vista Restaurant,
offering the finest cuisine in Sharn and
throughout the Five Nations. I am
your host, Evix ir'Marasha, and today
you are my guest. I'm often asked what
I'd recommend at the Celestial Vista.
All the food here is superb and
guaranteed pure by House Ghallanda.
The only thing I ever suggest is to not
look down—Enjoy your meal!"

Celestial Vista Restaurant

Azure District, Skyway • Proprietor: Evix ir'Marasha
All food proudly purified by House Ghallanda

DAYBREAK

15 Blood of Vol—Karrnathi sausage omelet with red pepper sauce
10 Vedbread*—Crusty cheese bread with onion butter
12 Elven Bread*—Cinnamon swirled with honey butter
8 Ashi Flatbread—Served with honey

MAINS AND SIDES

25 Eldeen Banquet—Loaded with vegetables
30 Pan-seared rabbit with Aundarian wood-nut sauce
35 Gold pheasant stuffed with sparkle mushrooms and rice
40 Dragon salmon in butter and dark wine sauce*
40 Beef Boranel with bread and mushroom dressing
25 Farmer's Stew
25 Thrice-poached eggs and sizzling pheasant
35 Fire-wrapped golden fish
35 Spiced pork and orange peppers
30 Hot-spiced chicken in panya leaves
40 Thrakel-seared beef in red sauce
30 Three-thrakel fish stew
15 Silvered vegetable skewers
45 Thrane Prime Sirloin
45 Karrnathi breaded veal

DESSERTS

8 Skyway Special—A light dessert omelet served atop whipped cream
7 Cremfels—A crème-filled crepe served with berries or syrup
6 Kettle fried spider and redeye berries
4 Beesh-berry sorbet
5 Silverfruit pie

BEVERAGES

5 Talenta Tal
8 Karrnathi Beer
8 Nightwood Ale
10 Aundarian Mursi
12 Kuryeva Gin
12 Sooka
10 Mror Ale

12 Lhazaar
6 Honey-milk
15 Arcanix Vineyards Fireburst Wine
20 Dark Orla-un Wine
22 Windshire Rainbow Wine
15 Aundarian Iltrayan Wine
12 Zil Brandy

4

HALFLING CUISINE

"It's hard to beat a meal in a halfling home, as long as you don't crack your head on the ceiling—good food and good stories in front of a nice, warm fire. If halflings had a shred of ambition, they might really amount to something."

—D&D *PLAYER'S HANDBOOK*

Halflings are creatures of comfort, with an intense love of peace, quiet, hearth, home, and, most of all, food. In stark contrast to humans, these simple pleasures are the sole ambition of this uniquely unambitious bunch. Whether living in the luxury of their halfling holes set in lush, pastoral landscapes or on the rocky road of adventure, halflings constantly alternate between two sentiments toward food: savoring and longing. When they are not doing one, they are undoubtedly doing the other. Unsurprisingly, food and drink are at the center of any halfling community, often providing the forum for their other favorite pastimes: fine conversation and storytelling. Add a pipe, some tea, and a comfortable chair, and a halfling has everything needed for lifelong fulfillment.

SMALL AND PRACTICAL
Standing roughly three feet tall, halflings are small and down-to-Oerth creatures, and so is their food—consisting of modest portions of delicious, unpretentious fare. But don't be fooled by the small plates, for halflings make up for it in quantity and variety of dishes. It is common for an ordinary halfling meal to consist of several courses, while a lavish feast may contain dozens of plates of fresh, simple foods bursting with earthy garden colors. However, halflings always favor taste and practicality over pomp and presentation.

When their lives are not in danger, halflings do nothing quickly—nothing except eat that is. While their meals can stretch for hours, often with one meal running right into another, their rate of consumption is something to behold, often outpacing their usually larger non-halfling companions more than two to one. Remarkably, they are not messy eaters, rather they use their extraordinary agility to eat stealthily, quickly, and cleanly, for they hate to see a crumb of anything go to waste. Need that lock picked now? Tell your halfling companions that a buffet waits immediately beyond and you'll marvel at the speed and precision at which they can work.

The concept of sharing is deeply rooted in halfling culture, whether it be imparting (sometimes hard-to-believe) stories of adventure or doling out that pot of stew they put on the stove. While they are largely unconcerned with formality and dining etiquette, they do strictly adhere to certain unwritten rules of hosting. The most notable of these is that, in a halfling dwelling, guests come first. This means the first serving of cheese, the first cut of meat, and seemingly unlimited portions of coffee, tea, biscuits, cake, and jams are made available to their guests, on demand. Unfortunately, this strong sense of hospitality sometimes goes unappreciated and unrewarded when boorish guests come by and deplete the larders of an overly polite halfling before the host can even sit or sample the meal for themselves.

KIND AND CURIOUS

Adventuring is not the true calling of most halflings—the typical variety usually referred to as "stouts" or "stronghearts"—but when it comes to food, they are as brave and adventurous as they come. Halflings will try virtually anything, from the new and experimental to the downright risky. They are not picky eaters, and their kind disposition shapes a nonjudgmental and forgiving, although not entirely undiscerning, palate. Can they find room for improvement? Sure, but is it really worth a trip all the way to the kitchen for the salt? They crave warm, rich flavors, both savory and sweet, such as cheddar, salted pork, vanilla, maple, walnuts, smoked almonds, butterscotch, and the like, usually served with a smooth, malty beverage. In a halfling household, just about anything can be enhanced by adding butter, eggs, and salt. It might be remarked that the diet of the average halfling will not result in an adventurer's waistline.

PASTORAL PLEASANTRIES

Most halflings, sometimes referred to as "hin," live in peaceful agrarian communities, which focus largely on farming, grove maintenance, and tending to private gardens—the pride and joy of any halfling home. A halfling garden is indeed something to behold as every square inch is optimized to produce a tasty herb, vegetable, or fruit that will enhance their next meal—farming and eating, longing and savoring. Halflings also raise livestock to assist with labor, transportation, and, of course, food. Pigs, chickens, cows, goats, and sheep are among the animals that often show up on the halfling table, but often in small quantities and with a high monetary, and sometimes emotional, price. With a few notable exceptions, such as the nomadic, dinosaur-riding Talenta Plains halflings of Khorvaire and the cannibalistic jungle variety of Athas, halflings tend to be a particularly cheerful and compassionate lot and hate to see any creature suffer. As such, it is not uncommon for a halfling farmer to befriend his livestock and end up buying his meat from one of his less merciful neighbors.

Halflings are also famed for their proficiency at cheesemaking. Be it hard, soft, sharp, or mild, halflings excel at the fine art of artisanal dairy preservation . . . and consumption. Any respectable halfling gathering is sure to boast an assortment of uniquely crafted cheeses. Moreover, halflings are proud bakers—skilled in all types of dough-making, ranging from fluffy morning buns to hearty loaves to delicately scrumptious desserts—who bake in quantities with their community in mind. For these small folk, desserts are a way of life.

Some particularly motivated or curious halflings do manage to leave the municipal boundaries of their villages and even hit the road of adventure. These wandering halflings, sometimes called "lightfoots" or "tallfellows," tend to do so in groups, journeying from hamlets to Hommlet by wagon or boat, usually in search of various curiosities, unfamiliar foods being first among them. It is said, "You can pull the halfling out of their shires, but you can't pull the shires out of the halfling." Such is the case with the adventuring types, carrying a strong sense of home with them wherever they go. And if you check their packs, you're bound to find more than a few effects of sentiment along with a disproportionate amount of food and ingredients from their hometowns.

Community Cheeses

It wouldn't be a halfling jamboree without a cauldron of community cheeses on the table for all to enjoy! This multi-cheese concoction is composed of two types, slowly melted with a spritz of wine in a fondue pot over an even, low heat. The key is to not overcook nor let the unique cheese flavors homogenize, which ensures that each bite is streaked with a surprising new taste combination. Usually presented with fruits, meat chunks, or cubed breads, this fondue is perfect for dagger-dipping. Just be sure to clean the blood off first!

PREPARE THE DIPPERS. Blanch the broccoli or cauliflower in boiling salted water until just tender, about 4 minutes. Drain and transfer to a bowl of ice water to stop the cooking. Then drain until dry or blot dry.

MAKE THE FONDUE. In a large bowl, mix the Gruyère and Emmental cheeses and set aside. In a small bowl, whisk ⅓ cup of the wine and the cornstarch to blend, and set aside.

In a heavy saucepan over medium heat, combine the remaining 1⅓ cups of wine and two of the garlic cloves and bring to a simmer. Remove the garlic, whisk the cornstarch mixture to recombine, add it to the pan, and stir constantly, until thickened, 15 to 30 seconds. Stir in the lemon juice.

Adjust the heat to medium-low and add about ½ cup of the cheese, stirring constantly but gently until fully melted. Repeat with the remaining cheeses in ½-cup increments, each time stirring until melted fully before adding more, about 8 minutes. Continue to cook, stirring constantly but gently, until the mixture is smooth and just begins to bubble, about 4 minutes more. Do not allow the mixture to boil; adjust the heat, if necessary. Add the Kirsch, nutmeg (if using), ½ teaspoon salt, and pepper to taste. Stir to combine. Taste and adjust the seasoning with additional salt and pepper, if necessary.

Meanwhile, warm a fondue pot with hot water, empty it, and dry it well. Rub the inside of the pot with the remaining garlic clove and pour in the fondue. Set the pot over a heat source, and serve at once with the dippers.

COOK'S NOTES

There is a lot of variation in the way cheeses melt. To increase your odds of a smooth outcome, use grated cheese at room temperature. Many experts advise using cheeses that are younger than a year old and avoiding those sourced from supermarket deli counters.

Cheeses can differ in saltiness, so season the fondue carefully. Start with ½ teaspoon kosher salt, and taste. If necessary, add more salt by the ¼ teaspoon.

SERVES 4 TO 6 AS A MAIN COURSE

DIPPERS

Broccoli and/or cauliflower, trimmed and cut into bite-size florets

Brussels sprouts, trimmed and halved

Roasted or steamed potatoes, cubed

Apples and/or pears, peeled, if desired, cored, and cut into bite-size pieces (toss with a small amount of fresh lemon juice to slow browning)

Ham steak, sautéed until lightly browned, and cut into bite-size pieces

Baguette or other good French bread, cut into bite-size pieces (each with some crust)

Raisin bread or dried fruit-nut bread or rolls, lightly toasted and cut into bite-size pieces

FONDUE

12 ounces Gruyère cheese, coarsely grated (4 cups, lightly packed), at room temperature

12 ounces Emmental cheese, coarsely grated (4 cups, lightly packed), at room temperature

1⅔ cups crisp, dry white wine

2 tablespoons cornstarch

3 garlic cloves, smashed

1 tablespoon fresh lemon juice

2 tablespoons Kirsch or Poire Williams

Pinch of freshly grated nutmeg (optional)

Kosher salt and freshly ground black or white pepper

Stuffed Egg-Battered Toast

There's nothing more comforting to a comfort-obsessed halfling than the warm intermingling scents of vanilla, maple, and walnuts filling their home. Thick slices of fresh-cut, fluffy bread are stuffed with cream cheese or mascarpone before getting egg-battered and pan-fried. The final touch is a drizzle of homemade marmalade or apricot syrup. This popular second morningfeast treat is customarily served after tea and satiates a halfling's cravings right up until the first midday meal.

SERVES 4

4 ounces (½ cup) mascarpone, at room temperature

¼ cup walnuts, finely chopped

2 teaspoons pure vanilla extract

4 (1-inch-thick) slices brioche or challah

2 eggs

½ cup whole milk

¼ teaspoon kosher salt

2 tablespoons unsalted butter

½ cup maple syrup

Confectioners' sugar for dusting

In a small bowl, stir together the mascarpone, walnuts, and vanilla.

Use a thin knife to cut a 2-inch-long slit through the side of each slice of brioche, creating a pocket. Gently open the pocket and spoon about 1 tablespoon of the mascarpone mixture into each slice.

In a pie dish or shallow bowl, whisk together the eggs, milk, and salt.

Melt 1 tablespoon of the butter in a large skillet over medium heat. Dip two stuffed slices into the egg mixture, turning to soak both sides and letting any excess batter drip back into the bowl. Place the slices in the skillet and cook for 2 to 3 minutes per side, until golden brown. Use a spatula to transfer the toasts to a warm plate. Repeat to cook the remaining two stuffed slices.

Meanwhile, warm the maple syrup in a small saucepan over low heat for a few minutes.

Dust the stuffed toast with confectioners' sugar, drizzle with the warm maple syrup, and serve.

COOK'S NOTES

Stuffing the mascarpone mixture into the thick slices of brioche requires a delicate touch (or small fingers). If creating a pocket in the side of each slice is too much trouble, you can also cut the bread ½ inch thick and spread the mascarpone in between two slices, like a sandwich.

Marmalade, heated over low heat in a pan, makes for a delectable syrup replacement.

CHICKEN-SOMETHING DUMPLINGS

Wouldn't you like to know the secret halfling ingredient that makes these magically delicious dough dollops melt in your mouth? Well, now you will! From the famed Hungry Halfling in Faerûn's Corm Orp to nearly every halfling suppertime table across the land, this hearty, velvety concoction laden with homemade drop dumplings is the coziest of comfort foods. There are countless variants of this dish, with each halfling household claiming to serve the finest, but nothing beats the thick-and-stewy classic—a robust poultry stock base, emboldened with the tastes of freshly picked veggies, parsley, and garlic all comingled with creamy dough.

TO MAKE THE STEW, sprinkle the chicken thighs all over with salt and pepper. In a large Dutch oven over medium-high heat, warm the olive oil until shimmering. Arrange half the chicken skin-side down in the Dutch oven, adjust the heat to medium, and cook, undisturbed, until the skin is browned, about 5 minutes. Turn over the chicken and continue to cook, undisturbed, until the second side is browned, about 5 minutes more; adjust the heat if it starts to scorch. Transfer the chicken to a large plate. Repeat with the remaining chicken thighs (and reserve any accumulated chicken fat). When the chicken is cool enough to handle, remove and discard the skin.

Thinly slice one of the leek halves. Cut the remaining three leek halves into 1-inch pieces.

Add the butter to the pot, return it to medium heat, and melt and swirl in the pot to coat. Add the thinly sliced leeks, bay leaves, thyme, and ½ teaspoon salt and cook, stirring constantly, until the leeks are softened, about 2 minutes. Add the garlic and flour and continue to cook, stirring, for about 2 minutes more. Add the sherry and bring to a simmer, stirring and scraping the pan bottom to loosen and dissolve any browned bits. Continue to simmer, stirring, until the liquid is thickened and slightly reduced, about 1 minute more. Gradually add the broth, stirring vigorously to incorporate it smoothly.

CONTINUED ON PAGE 124 →

SERVES 4

CHICKEN STEW

6 bone-in, skin-on chicken thighs (2 to 2½ pounds)

Kosher salt and freshly ground black pepper

2 teaspoons olive oil

2 leeks, white and light green parts, halved lengthwise

2 tablespoons unsalted butter

2 bay leaves

2 teaspoons finely chopped fresh thyme, or 1 teaspoon dried

5 garlic cloves, finely chopped

3 tablespoons all-purpose flour

½ cup dry sherry, such as Amontillado

2 cups low-sodium chicken broth

2 carrots, peeled and diagonally cut into 1-inch slices

2 celery stalks, trimmed and diagonally cut into 1-inch slices

⅓ cup chopped fresh parsley

INGREDIENTS CONTINUED →

> *"The food served there is as good and hearty as popular lore credits halflings for. (The chicken dumplings are superb.)"*
>
> **—ED GREENWOOD**, *VOLO'S GUIDE TO THE SWORD COAST*

CHICKEN-SOMETHING DUMPLINGS, CONTINUED

DUMPLINGS

1¾ cups all-purpose flour

2 teaspoons baking powder

2 teaspoons onion powder

1 teaspoon kosher salt

Freshly ground black pepper

6 scallions, green and white parts, thinly sliced

2 tablespoons unsalted butter, cut into 4 pieces

2 tablespoons olive oil or reserved chicken fat (from browning the chicken)

¾ cup whole milk

Add the chicken thighs with any of the accumulated juices to the pot and return to a simmer. Adjust the heat to very low, cover, and simmer gently until the chicken is cooked through and very tender, about 1 hour, turning the chicken pieces over after about 30 minutes. Transfer the chicken to a plate.

When the chicken is cool enough to handle, remove the meat from the bones and shred it into large chunks. Remove the bay leaves from the pot, add the shredded chicken, ½ teaspoon salt, and a few grinds of pepper; stir to mix. Over medium-high heat, return to a simmer. Taste and adjust the seasoning with salt and pepper, if necessary.

MEANWHILE, MAKE THE DUMPLINGS. Whisk together the flour, baking powder, onion powder, salt, and a few grinds of pepper in a bowl. Add the scallions and toss to combine. In a microwave-safe bowl, microwave the butter and olive oil (or reserved chicken fat, if you have any), stopping to swirl occasionally, to melt the butter. Add the milk and continue to microwave on high until the mixture is just warm (do not overheat), about 1½ minutes. Add the warmed milk mixture to the flour mixture. With a wooden spoon or fork, mix until incorporated and uniformly moist (the mixture should look like a wet, shaggy dough).

To finish the chicken and cook the dumplings, add the carrots, celery, 1-inch leek pieces, and most of the parsley to the stew and stir to incorporate it. Using a soup spoon, drop twelve golf ball–size portions of dumpling dough into the pot, placing them about ½ inch apart (drop eight around the perimeter and four in the center). Adjust the heat to low, cover, and cook undisturbed until the dumplings are puffed and cooked through, and a toothpick inserted into them comes out clean, 15 to 20 minutes.

Ladle the stew into bowls, allowing three dumplings per portion. Sprinkle each with some of the remaining parsley and serve.

Hogs in Bedrolls

Few things put a spring in a halfling's step quite like the buttery-sausage scent of freshly baked hogs in bedrolls wafting through the village. As curious as they are resourceful, halflings have a knack for creating new culinary combinations of things they love to eat—in this case, savory sausages and flaky pastries. Diminutive, smoked pork-and-beef bangers are snugly rolled up into salty dough "bedrolls" until only their "heads" are poking out. The expert maneuver is to brush these little snacks with a thin egg wash before popping them in the oven, ensuring a glossy shine and a boost of color. And slathering them with butter once they are cooked is a truly tasty touch. Hogs in bedrolls might just be the perfect finger food for any size halfling gathering.

Preheat the oven to 400°F. Line two large rimmed baking sheets with parchment paper or nonstick (silicone) liners.

On a lightly floured work surface, unfold or unroll the puff pastry. If necessary, use a rolling pin to gently roll it flat (take care not to press too hard, which compresses the layers, decreasing its puff when baked). Cut as many 2-inch squares as you have cocktail franks. Lay each frank diagonally on a square, fold the two opposite corners up and over the frank to meet at the top, and press or pinch them to adhere. Arrange them about 1 inch apart on the prepared baking sheets.

In a small bowl, beat the egg with 1 tablespoon water and brush the top and sides of each bedroll with the mixture. Bake until the bedrolls are browned, puffed, and crisp, about 17 minutes, rotating the sheets 180 degrees and switching racks halfway through baking. Set the baking sheets on wire racks and let the bedrolls cool for about 5 minutes. Serve hot, with ketchup, mustard, barbecue sauce, or steak sauce on the side for dipping (if desired).

MAKES ABOUT 40 ROLLS

1 to 2 sheet(s) frozen all-butter puff pastry (see Cook's Note), thawed according to package directions

1 (12-ounce) package cocktail franks

1 egg

Ketchup, mustard, barbecue sauce, or steak sauce for dipping (optional)

COOK'S NOTES

The measurements of different brands of puff pastry sheets differ, but most include two sheets.

Many cocktail franks measure about 1½ inches in length. If yours differ, adjust the size of your puff pastry squares accordingly, keeping them about ½ inch longer and wider than the franks. If you can't find cocktail franks, buy the most slender hot dogs you can and cut them into 1½-inch lengths. If the hot dogs are fatter than cocktail franks, though, you may have to adjust the size of your puff squares.

MELTED CHEESES WITH CHUNKY TOMATO BROTH

Halflings not only know their cheese, they also boast innumerable ways to prepare it. Bread, buttered on the outside, is layered with strips of cheese, sprinkled with seasoning, and pan-fried, before being sliced into strips, or "dippers," for soup dunking. The recipe itself is quite simple (and really just an excuse to eat more cheese)! Sometimes served spicy, these sandwiches are often dashed with dill, nutmeg, basil, or the like, depending on the mood of the chef. The same goes for the accompanying soup, commonly a chunky tomato but occasionally a smooth red pepper puree. It's always served warm, more as a sort of dipping sauce that can be guzzled once the cheeses have disappeared. One of the simplest midday recipes in the halfling repertoire, melted cheeses have also been heavily adopted by humans across the land, with the dish adorning countless tavern menus.

MAKE THE SOUP. In a large saucepan or Dutch oven over medium heat, melt the butter. Add the onion, bay leaf, and ½ teaspoon salt and cook, stirring frequently, until soft and light golden, about 5 minutes. Add the brown sugar and tomato paste and cook, stirring, until fragrant, about 1 minute. Add the chicken broth and rice. Reserve three tomatoes and add the remainder with the juices, adjust the heat to medium-high, and bring to a simmer. Adjust the heat to medium-low, cover, and continue to simmer, stirring occasionally, until the rice is very tender, about 20 minutes. Remove the bay leaf.

In a countertop blender, or with an immersion blender, puree the tomato mixture until smooth; return the pureed mixture to the pot. Chop the reserved tomatoes, add to the soup, and stir. Taste and adjust the seasoning with additional salt, if necessary, and pepper. Cover and keep warm over very low heat.

TO MAKE THE MELTED CHEESE SANDWICHES, set a large nonstick or cast-iron griddle over medium-low heat.

Spread about 2 teaspoons of the softened butter on one side of four slices of the bread, all the way to the edges. Place them on the work surface buttered-sides down. Top each slice with about ½ cup of grated cheese. Spread the remaining softened butter on one side of each of the remaining four slices of bread. Place them on the sandwiches buttered-sides up. Transfer the sandwiches to the griddle or skillet and cook until golden brown and crisp, 3 to 5 minutes on each side. Transfer the sandwiches to a cutting board and cut crosswise into four or five strips.

Serve the tomato broth and melted cheeses together, sprinkling each bowl of broth with the chopped herbs.

SERVES 4

TOMATO BROTH

2 tablespoons salted butter

1 large onion, finely chopped

1 bay leaf

Kosher salt

1 tablespoon light brown sugar

1 tablespoon tomato paste

4 cups low-sodium chicken broth

2 tablespoons long-grain white rice

1 (28-ounce) can peeled whole tomatoes

Freshly ground black pepper

MELTED CHEESE SANDWICHES

6 tablespoons salted butter, softened

8 (½-inch-thick) slices white or multigrain French, Italian, or sandwich bread

8 ounces firm or semifirm cheese (such as a young Cheddar, Colby, Monterey Jack, Fontina, Havarti, Gouda, or Baby Swiss), coarsely grated

1½ tablespoons chopped fresh parsley, dill, or chives for garnish

HALFLING OATMEAL SWEET NIBBLES

Dense with oats, chocolate chips, and butterscotch, these diminutive cookies are perfect for halfling hands . . . and the stomachs of everyone. The secret is to pull each batch from the oven a minute before they are done cooking and allow them to finish on the tray to ensure a golden outside and an extra-gooey core. Indeed, these nibbles are everything a halfling looks for at the dinner table: rich, delicious flavors and speedy preparation (just in time for tea!).

MAKES ABOUT 45 COOKIES

1½ cups all-purpose flour

2 cups rolled oats

1 teaspoon baking soda

½ teaspoon kosher salt

1½ cups packed light brown sugar

1 cup unsalted butter, at room temperature

1 egg, beaten

2 teaspoons pure vanilla extract

1 cup semisweet chocolate chips

1 cup butterscotch chips

Preheat the oven to 350°F. Line two large rimmed baking sheets with parchment paper or nonstick (silicone) liners.

In a bowl, stir together the flour, oats, baking soda, and salt.

In a large bowl, beat together the brown sugar and butter until light and creamy. Mix in the egg and vanilla. Add the flour mixture and stir until incorporated. Stir in the chocolate chips and butterscotch chips.

Scoop the dough by the rounded tablespoon and place about 2 inches apart on the prepared baking sheets. You'll need to bake a second batch of cookies because they won't all fit on the two baking sheets. (It's okay to reuse the parchment paper.)

Bake for 15 minutes, rotating the positions of the baking sheets halfway through, until the cookies are golden brown and a little darker around the edges. Let cool on the baking sheets for a few minutes, then transfer to a wire rack to cool completely. Repeat with the remaining dough. Store in an airtight container at room temperature for up to 3 days.

──────── COOK'S NOTE ────────

Smaller cookies will affect the cook time and later batches will cook noticeably faster if you are using the same baking sheet. For softer cookies, try cutting the cook time by a quarter.

Lluirwood Salad

Located along the northern border of the former halfling nation of Luiren was the Lluirwood of southeast Faerûn. Sometimes called "the Longforest," due to its lengthy expanse, this dense woodland was the native homeland of three groups of halfling who once foraged the thick foliage in search of delectable forest treats. After the Hin Ghostwars, the Lluirwood was mostly abandoned by halflings and subsequently inhabited by ill-tempered monsters that wandered in from the Toadsquat Mountains to the north. But even after generations, hungry hin from the coastal cities of Luiren still craved those tasty forest flavors and paid adventurers handsomely to extract its ingredients. Prior to the Spellplague, which submerged all of Luiren, this sweet and savory salad, made up of whole-leaf spinach, dried cranberries, candied pecans, and spring cheese, topped with a tangy vinaigrette dressing, would anchor the menus of taverns from Beluir to Shoun—a perfect starter to first or second evenfeast.

To make the vinaigrette, in a large salad bowl, whisk together the vinegar, lemon juice, mustard, shallot, ½ teaspoon salt, and pepper to taste. Vigorously whisk in the olive oil to blend. Taste and adjust the seasoning with additional salt and pepper, if necessary. Reserve 1½ tablespoons.

Add the spinach to the bowl and toss to coat. Add ¼ teaspoon salt, pepper to taste, the goat cheese, most of the nuts, and most of the cranberries; toss to combine. Sprinkle with the remaining nuts and cranberries, drizzle with the reserved 1½ tablespoons vinaigrette, and serve.

SERVES 4

2½ teaspoons sherry vinegar

1 teaspoon fresh lemon juice

¾ teaspoon Dijon mustard

2 tablespoons minced shallot

Kosher salt and freshly ground black pepper

¼ cup extra-virgin olive oil

8 cups packed fresh baby spinach leaves (about 4½ ounces)

Kosher salt and freshly ground black pepper

1 (4- to 5-ounce) log fresh goat cheese, crumbled

⅔ cup candied or spiced pecans or other nuts, chopped or broken into pieces

½ cup dried cranberries

EVERYTHING SOUP

This hearty soup was named for the halfling tradition of frantically raiding their pantries and gardens in nervous anticipation of hosting guests. Sometimes referred to as "Welcome Soup," this stew is a meal in itself, brimming with a colorful medley of vegetables (including up to four different colors of carrots!), green beans, peas, sweet flint corn, red bell peppers, and pulled poultry in a flavorful broth. It should be noted that some adventuresome halflings boldly mix chicken and turkey stock for extra oomph. This substantial soup will warm you to the core. And it cures curses, or so it's been rumored.

SERVES 6

6 tablespoons unsalted butter

2 teaspoons finely chopped fresh rosemary

2 garlic cloves, finely chopped

Kosher salt

1 large yellow onion, chopped

3 rainbow carrots, peeled and diagonally cut into ¾-inch slices

1 red bell pepper, cored, seeded, and cut into ¾-inch pieces

2 large bay leaves

1½ teaspoons finely chopped fresh thyme, or ¾ teaspoon dried

5 cups low-sodium chicken broth

1 Yukon gold potato (about 6 ounces), peeled and cut into ¾-inch cubes

4 ounces green beans, trimmed and cut into 1-inch pieces

1 small leek, white and light green parts, halved lengthwise, thinly sliced, rinsed thoroughly, and drained

¾ cup frozen corn kernels

1½ cups (8 ounces) bite-size or shredded skinless pieces of home-cooked or rotisserie chicken

Freshly ground black pepper

In a small skillet over medium heat, melt 3 tablespoons of the butter. Add the rosemary, garlic, and a tiny pinch of salt and cook, stirring, until fragrant, about 1 minute. Remove from the heat and set the skillet aside for the butter to infuse.

In a Dutch oven or large saucepan over medium-high heat, melt the remaining 3 tablespoons butter. Add the onion, carrots, red pepper, bay leaves, thyme, and 1 teaspoon salt and cook, stirring, until the vegetables soften, about 5 minutes. Adjust the heat to medium-low, cover, and continue cooking, stirring occasionally, until the vegetables have released their juices, about 8 minutes. Add the broth and potato, adjust the heat to medium-high, and bring the liquid to a simmer. Adjust the heat to very low, cover, and simmer until the potato is barely tender, about 5 minutes. Add the green beans, adjust the heat to medium-high, and return the liquid to a simmer. Adjust the heat to very low, cover, and simmer until the green beans are barely tender, about 3 minutes more. Add the leek, corn, chicken, ¾ teaspoon salt, and a few grinds of pepper; adjust the heat to medium-high; and return the liquid to a simmer. Adjust the heat to very low, cover, and simmer until the potato is fully tender, the green beans are tender-crisp, the leeks are wilted, and the corn and chicken are heated through, about 3 minutes more. Remove the bay leaves. Taste and adjust the seasoning with additional salt and pepper, if necessary.

Return the rosemary-garlic butter to medium heat to melt. Strain the butter through a fine-mesh strainer. Serve the soup, drizzling a teaspoon or two of the flavored butter on the surface of each serving.

Honeyed Ham with Pineapple Gravy

When it's time for a holiday feast, honeyed ham is the first dish in a halfling's oven. A large ham is brushed with layer upon layer of a local honey, brown sugar, and pineapple juice glaze for maximum sweetness before being set in the oven. And while the simmering scent of slow-cooking pork fills the homestead, a halfling gets to work on the accompanying pineapple gravy, a chunky and tangy sauce to drown your beast and starches in. It should be noted that this recipe goes just as well with wild boar, if you are inclined to catch one.

Remove the ham from the refrigerator 1½ to 2 hours before cooking so that it starts at room temperature.

Preheat the oven to 300°F with a rack in the lower-middle of the oven. Cover a large roasting pan or rimmed baking sheet with foil. Set a roasting rack in the roasting pan and cover that with foil, shiny-side up, leaving overhangs sufficient to fully wrap the ham once it's on the rack. Position the ham cut-side down on the rack, cover with the overhanging foil, and crimp the edges to seal the ham. Bake until the ham registers about 120°F on an instant-read thermometer, 3 to 3 ½ hours.

At around the 3-hour mark, in a skillet over medium-high heat, bring the pineapple juice to a boil. Continue to boil until the juice is reduced to 1 cup, 8 to 10 minutes. Pour off and reserve ⅔ cup of the reduced juice for the sauce.

Add ½ cup of the honey, the brown sugar, 2 teaspoons mustard, cloves, and ½ teaspoon pepper, to the remaining ⅓ cup reduced juice in the skillet and whisk to combine.

Remove the ham from the oven and adjust the oven temperature to 400°F. Peel back the foil and, working carefully with the hot ham, pour as much of the accumulated ham juices as possible into a large measuring cup or bowl and set aside. Brush half the pineapple juice mixture evenly over the exposed surfaces of the ham (don't worry about the cut side). Leaving the foil open, bake until glossy and beginning to caramelize, about 15 minutes. Brush the remaining mixture over the ham and continue baking, again until glossy and caramelized, about 8 minutes more.

CONTINUED ON PAGE 136 →

SERVES 10 TO 14

1 small (10-pound) spiral-sliced, bone-in ham, preferably shank-end

2 cups unsweetened pineapple juice

¾ cup honey

⅓ cup packed light brown sugar

2 teaspoons Dijon mustard, plus 1 tablespoon

¼ teaspoon ground cloves, or to taste

Freshly ground black pepper

2 tablespoons unsalted butter

1 shallot, finely chopped

2 teaspoons finely chopped fresh thyme

Kosher salt

1 tablespoon cornstarch

1 cup finely chopped fresh pineapple

Honeyed Ham with Pineapple Gravy,

CONTINUED

Remove the ham from the oven and again working carefully, pour as much of the accumulated ham juices as possible into the bowl with the first batch (you may have as much as 1½ cups) and set aside. Fold the foil back up over the ham to tent loosely and let rest for 15 minutes.

In a saucepan over medium heat, melt the butter. Add the shallot, thyme, and ½ teaspoon salt and cook, stirring, until the shallot softens, about 2 minutes. Add the ⅔ cup reserved reduced pineapple juice, the remaining ¼ cup honey, and remaining 1 tablespoon mustard. Whisk to combine and bring to a simmer, about 2 minutes.

In a bowl or measuring cup, whisk the cornstarch and ⅔ cup of the reserved ham juices until uniform. Add to the saucepan and cook, stirring, until thickened, about 1 minute. Add the chopped pineapple and pepper to taste and cook, stirring, to heat the sauce through, 1 to 2 minutes more. Taste and adjust the seasoning with additional salt and pepper, if necessary. Carve the ham and serve with the warm sauce.

HEARTLANDS ROSE APPLE AND BLACKBERRY PIE

As the story goes, a hungry halfling returned from her hillside stroll with a heavy basket of crisp rose apples and plump blackberries. In typical indecisive halfling fashion, she couldn't decide which to fill her pie with . . . so she chose both, and thus this legendary halfling dessert pie was born. A thick handmade crust and a flaky, buttery top blanket a tart and tasty rose apple (nearly any apple suffices, season pending, of course) and blackberry filling with spiced ground accents. Some halflings even dust their crust with a white Cheddar that melts for a unique flavor, but all of them agree that it would be a sin to serve this without a scoop of freshly whipped sweet cream.

In a large microwave-safe bowl, mix ⅓ cup of the sugar, the cinnamon, 1 tablespoon of the cornstarch, and ¼ teaspoon salt. Add the apples and toss gently to combine. Microwave the mixture until the apples just begin to soften and release juices, 7 to 10 minutes, stirring gently with a flexible spatula every 2 to 3 minutes. Cool to room temperature, about 30 minutes.

On a floured work surface or sheet of parchment paper, roll out one piece of pastry into a 12-inch circle. Transfer the pastry into a deep-dish pie plate, fitting it in by gently lifting the edge of the pastry with one hand while lightly pressing it into the plate bottom and up the sides with the other hand; leave an overhang of about 1 inch. Refrigerate until the pastry is firm, about 30 minutes.

Preheat the oven to 425°F with a large baking sheet on a rack in the lower-middle position in the oven.

In a bowl, mix together ⅓ cup of the sugar, the remaining 2 tablespoons cornstarch, and a tiny pinch of salt. Add the blackberries and gently toss to coat. Add the lemon juice and gently fold until the sugar mixture is moistened and syrupy. Spread the blackberry mixture evenly into the dough-lined pie plate and scatter the butter pieces over the berry mixture. With a slotted spoon, spoon the apples evenly over the berries and mound them slightly in the center. Pour about half of the exuded juices over the apples.

CONTINUED ON PAGE 140 →

MAKES ONE 9-INCH DEEP-DISH PIE

⅔ cup plus 1 tablespoon sugar

½ teaspoon ground cinnamon

3 tablespoons cornstarch

Kosher salt

3½ pounds (about 6) baking apples (such as Golden Delicious, Ginger Gold, Jonathan, Jonagold, Honeycrisp, Cortland, or Empire), peeled, quartered, cored, and cut lengthwise into ¼-inch slices

Pastry for 2 double-crust pies, thawed if frozen and rested at room temperature until pliable without cracking, about 30 minutes

12 ounces (about 2½ cups) blackberries, rinsed

1 tablespoon fresh lemon juice

1½ tablespoons unsalted butter, cut into small pieces

1 egg

Lightly sweetened whipped cream for serving (optional)

HEARTLANDS ROSE APPLE
AND BLACKBERRY PIE,
CONTINUED

On a floured work surface or sheet of parchment paper, roll out the second piece of pastry into a 12-inch circle. Place the pastry over the apples, leaving an overhang of about 1 inch. Using kitchen shears, cut evenly through both layers of overhanging pastry, leaving an overhang of about ½ inch. Fold the pastry under itself so that the edge of the fold is even with the edge of the pie plate and flute the pastry using your thumb and forefinger, or crimp it with the tines of a fork, to seal.

In a small bowl, beat the egg with 1 tablespoon water and brush onto the top of the pie (you'll probably have some left over). Sprinkle the remaining 1 tablespoon sugar evenly over the top. Set the pie on the preheated baking sheet and bake until the top is light golden brown, about 25 minutes. Adjust the temperature to 375°F, rotate the baking sheet 180 degrees, and continue baking until the crust is golden brown, 25 to 30 minutes more.

Set the pie on a wire rack and let it cool to room temperature, about 2 hours. Serve with whipped cream, if desired.

HONEY-DRIZZLED CREAM PUFFS

Stuffed with vanilla custard, these delectable treats deservedly grace every halfling dessert spread from Amn up to Neverwinter and beyond. The crispy hollow pastry puffs, which can be prepared days in advance, are a treat alone, but not enough can be said about the custard filling—a dense, velvety blend of cream, vanilla, and honey. While this custard is a wonderful filling or topping for any dessert, best applied with a straight-tipped pastry bag, it's perfectly normal to eat it by the spoonful as well (or so it's been reported). If you don't drizzle these puffs with a fine local honey, you are doing it wrong.

MAKE THE PUFFS. Preheat the oven to 425°F with a rack in the middle of the oven. Line a large rimmed baking sheet with parchment paper or a nonstick (silicone) baking mat.

In a small bowl, beat the separated egg yolk with 1 teaspoon water and set aside. In a second small bowl, beat the separated egg white with the remaining two whole eggs and the vanilla and set aside.

In a saucepan over medium-high heat, combine the water, milk, butter, sugar, and salt and cook, stirring, until the butter has melted and the mixture is on the verge of boiling, 2 to 4 minutes. Remove from the heat, add the flour all at once, and, with a wooden spoon, beat the mixture until a cohesive ball forms. Return the pan to medium-low heat and continue beating the dough, using a smearing motion, for 3 minutes, until the dough is very smooth and slightly drier.

Scrape the dough into a food processor and, with the feed tube open, process for about 10 seconds to cool it slightly. With the motor running, slowly pour in the beaten eggs through the feed tube and process until they are absorbed, about 10 seconds. Stop and scrape down the sides of the food processor bowl, then continue processing until the paste becomes thick, smooth, and sticky, about 15 seconds more.

Scrape the paste into a large plastic bag and, using your hands or a bench scraper, push it into one lower corner of the bag. Cut off ½ inch from the very corner of the bag and pipe the paste onto the prepared baking sheet in 2-inch mounds, leaving at least a ½-inch space around each one.

CONTINUED ON PAGE 142 →

MAKES ABOUT 12 CREAM PUFFS

PUFFS

1 egg, separated, plus 2 whole eggs

1 teaspoon pure vanilla extract

⅓ cup water

3 tablespoons whole milk

5 tablespoons unsalted butter, cut into several pieces

1½ tablespoons sugar

½ teaspoon kosher salt

⅔ cup all-purpose flour, sifted

FILLING

1⅓ cups heavy cream, cold

3 tablespoons honey

⅓ cup crème fraîche, cold

¾ teaspoon pure vanilla extract

HONEY-DRIZZLED CREAM PUFFS,
CONTINUED

Dip a spoon into cold water and use the back of the spoon to even out the shape and smooth the surface of the mounds. Using a pastry brush, brush each mound with a small portion of the reserved egg yolk mixture.

Bake for 15 minutes, then adjust the oven temperature to 375°F and continue baking until golden brown and firm, 7 to 9 minutes more.

Remove the puffs from the oven and, with the tip of a paring knife, cut a ¾-inch slit into the side of each puff to release steam. Turn off the oven, place the puffs on the baking sheet, return to the oven, prop the door open with a wooden spoon, and allow the puffs to dry, until the centers are barely moist and the exteriors are crisp, about 40 minutes. Transfer the puffs to a wire rack to cool to room temperature.

TO MAKE THE FILLING, with a stand mixer fitted with the whisk attachment, a handheld electric mixer, or a whisk, beat the cream until it is softly whipped, adding the honey once the cream has thickened. Add the crème fraîche and vanilla and continue to beat until the mixture holds very stiff peaks.

Just before serving, cut the puffs in half. Fill each bottom half with about ¼ cup of the filling, position the top halves on the filling, arrange on a serving platter, drizzle with honey, and serve.

COOK'S NOTE

To enhance both the flavor and stability of the filling, add crème fraîche to the whipped cream.

The Green Dragon Inn

Cargo Street, River Quarter · Free City of Greyhawk

Food

Eggs, boiled and spiced	2 sp		Mutton meatloaf	7 sp
Sausage/humble pie	2 sp		Wolf steak	1 gp
"Orc" Bacon*, thick cut (three slices)	1 sp		Venison, marinated in red wine and spices	1 gp
Muffins with berries	5 cp		Broiled crayfish in butter and scallions	1 gp
Honey butter	1 cp		Spit-roast stuffed goose	1 gp
Smoked Okerlund Cheese Wheel	3 sp		Pleasures of the deep in red broth and sherry	1 gp
Perrelander Cheese	3 sp		Barrier Peaks Surrogate Steaks"	10 sp
Nutbread loaf	7 cp		D'Amberville Onion Soup*	1 gp
Fried bread and spices	5 cp		Heroes' Feast* (only available Fridays when cleric is present)	20 sp
Greens with garlic	1 sp			
Soup, leek and boar	1 sp		The Endless Platter — river eels, smoked, all you can eat	3 sp
Fried mushroom in garlic sauce	1 sp			
Quij's Plate (sausage and potatoes)	2 sp		Bread pudding, warm in milk and butter	3 sp
Boar ragout (turnips and onions)	5 sp			
Traveler's Stew*	5 sp		Berry tart	3 sp
Steak and kidney pie	5 sp		Mincemeat stars	3 sp
Veal, breaded with gravy	1 gp		Ice cake	3 sp
Trout, stuffed or as you like it	1 gp		Gingerbread man, Greyhawk style*	2 sp
Poached salmon	1 gp			

Drinks

All drinks served by the pint unless it says otherwise

Ale	2 sp		Velunan Fireamber Wine	1 pp
Stout	1 sp		Mulled wine*	1 ep
Milk stout	1 sp		Brandy, local (gill)	1 ep
Honey mead	1 ep		Keoish Brandy, imported (gill)	1 sp
House Wine	1 ep		Urnst Brandy, special aged (gill)	1 sp
Keoish Golden Wine	15 sp		Ulik Elixir Liquer (1/2 gill)	5 sp
Sundish Lilac Wine	5 ep		Hill Giant Black Wine	5 sp
Urnst White Wine	1 gp		Purple Grapemash No. 3	3 sp
Celene Ruby Wine	2 sp		Herbal tea	5 cp
Furyondian Emerald Pale Wine	4 sp		Owlbear milk, served warm or cold	5 cp

Rooms

shared · 1 sp   private · 2 gp   suite · 5 gp

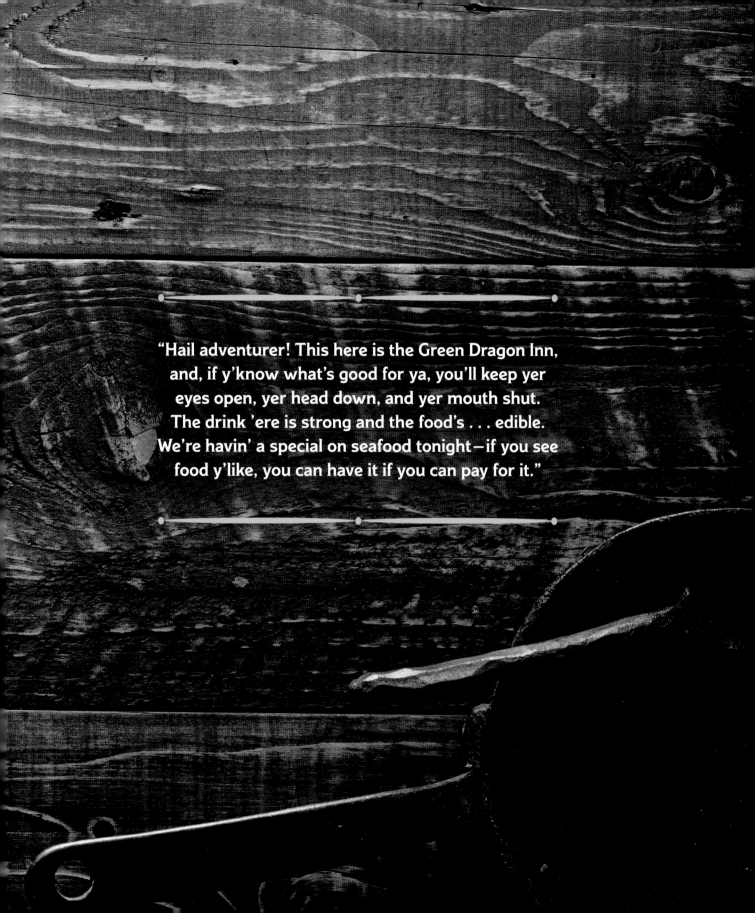

"Hail adventurer! This here is the Green Dragon Inn, and, if y'know what's good for ya, you'll keep yer eyes open, yer head down, and yer mouth shut. The drink 'ere is strong and the food's . . . edible. We're havin' a special on seafood tonight—if you see food y'like, you can have it if you can pay for it."

5

UNCOMMON CUISINE

"A visit to one of the great cities in the worlds of Dungeons & Dragons—Waterdeep, the Free City of Greyhawk, or even the uncanny Sigil, the City of Doors—overwhelms the senses. Voices chatter in countless different languages. The smells of cooking in dozens of different cuisines mingle with the odors of crowded streets.... Scattered among the members of these more common races are the true exotics: a hulking dragonborn here, pushing his way through the crowd, and a sly tiefling there, lurking in the shadows with mischief in her eyes. A group of gnomes laughs as one of them activates a clever wooden toy that moves on its own accord."

—D&D *PLAYER'S HANDBOOK*

The vast worlds of the multiverse are brimming with humanoid life of all shapes, sizes, and creeds. Yet despite the bountiful biological diversity of the planes, some groups are simply more common than others: namely humans, elves, dwarves, and halflings. Their sheer numbers set the culinary standard of the realms; but off the beaten path, a panoply of less prevalent cultures cut their own paths through the world of food. From the proud dragonborn and the outcast tiefling to the steadfast warforged and the angelic aasimar, these rare folk represent vibrant and powerful cultures that make their mark in the worlds where they may be found.

Frequently referred to as "uncommon," these humanoids can blend into the multi-cultural cosmopolitan cities of the planets they populate. However, they are often confronted by harmful social stigmas in the outlying hamlets of some of the more xenophobic communities, which even go so far as to deem them "monsters." In such archaic places, even groups as ubiquitous as dwarves and halflings can be met with nervous xenophobia. While the great urban centers of the multiverse worlds, such as Waterdeep, Sharn, or Greyhawk, readily welcome residents from far-off lands, their metropolitan cultures are simply too entrenched to accept much outside influence. Without a proper community in place, often all that exists of these uncommon cultures is what each solitary individual brings with them. And while human cultures receive many outside newcomers, it is rare to see a human adventurous enough to live among these more remote civilizations.

Cultural dissimilarities create unjust disadvantages, and to make things worse, basic physical differences, such as the size and shape of abodes, furniture, and domestic items, are common significant challenges facing those that wade into human-centric civilization. The broad-winged aarakocra, accustomed to a large nest, might struggle for a good night's sleep on an inn's down-bedded mattress, while reclusive giant-kin such as firbolgs or goliaths, may find it near impossible to comfortably dine at a human-made table.

UNCOMMON TASTES
From rustic campfires to the courts of kings, these very same differences apply to all matters of the kitchen; be it cooking utensils, cookware, raw ingredients, and even portions. For less common groups, finding familiar cuisine on a pub menu is incredibly rare if not impossible. Only the most cultured and enlightened humans, elves, and halflings experiment with these unique dishes and their uncommon preparation

techniques. However, any adventurous eater is sure to be rewarded with delicious options that excite the senses. Tiefling hellhound marrow might require a jaunt to the nine hells, but it's worth it; whereas the dragonborn delicacy of flambé crispy halfling flesh would surely land you into trouble in most towns (no pain, no gain). And the triton's live seafood bouillabaisse surely isn't for everyone.

The meals of these humanoids are far more than merely edible and nutritious—they often exhibit an almost alchemical explosion of flavors and textures, despite the fact they usually comprise commonplace ingredients. A chef with a cultured palate might be inspired to incorporate some of these ingredients, or utilize foreign preparation techniques, to create beautiful and novel culinary hybrids.

Nonetheless, it is essential to look past differences and toward what unites them. These humanoids usually occupy the very same ecosystems as other groups; they hunt the same woods, fish the same waters, and harvest the same plains. While territorial boundaries may put them at odds, the core shopping lists often remain essentially the same. But also, a word of warning: Some foods, spices, and ingredients from these uncommon groups can seriously injure, kill, or curse a humanoid. So, be wary, fair traveler (especially of the tiefling fiendspice and fire fruit)! It is best to navigate these distinctive menus with a mind that is as much cautious as it is open.

While it would be impossible to analyze every culture and creed within the vast multiverse, the following represent what you might call the *most common* uncommons, each with their own distinct culinary traditions and notable contributions.

DRAGONBORN: MEDIUM RARE

The dragonborn philosophy around food is a simple one: kill it, grill it, eat it. Even though their exact ancestral heritage is open for debate, one thing that is agreed upon is that they are closely related to dragons (or in some tales descended directly from draconic gods) and their tastes are generally consistent with dragon fare: meat—charred, smoky, or raw—garnished by occasional grains and vegetables. However, in stark contrast to their more solitary dragon cousins, dragonborn are humanoids who live in tight-knit, clan-based societies that prioritize honor, conduct (evil or good), and the welfare of the community above all things. As a result, dragonborn meals are communal affairs steeped in a surprising amount of formality and tradition. Huge family-style platters of assorted meats adorn fireproof, stone tables; while in some clans, dragonborn servers walk the feast halls with carving knives and heavy skewers of grilled or barbecued meats, serving up veritable buffets of generous savory chops.

The dragonborn's innate drive for self-improvement and excellence permeates all aspects of their culture, including its dining and cuisine. Accordingly, most dragonborn chefs have spent their entire lives in the pursuit of excellence in the culinary arts, and when it comes to meat, they've got it mastered, whether prepared cooked or raw. But always make sure to ask what's on the plate before you try it; in many dragonborn cultures, humanoid meat is not "off the table."

GNOME: THE FORGOTTEN FOLK

The planets of the multiverse are teeming with apex predators and towering, war-hungry humanoids, but gnomes, the most petite of the pervasive folk, thrive by embracing their emotions and harnessing their curiosity. Gnomes are nimble and clever, with an uncanny ability to blend into any environ, allowing them to skillfully avert the attention of would-be aggressors. They are inquisitive tinkerers at heart who have quietly managed to coexist with the taller bipedal kind, often benefitting from their hubris. Although gnomes can live for centuries, they embrace each day to the fullest, finding comfort in displaying their broad spectrum of emotions. They are resourceful and thoughtful, especially when it comes to cuisine where they skillfully maximize natural and readily available ingredients into small-portioned, serviceable dishes.

Gnomes are social eaters, favoring sit-down, multicourse meals, yet they display limited variety in their recipes usually due to a lack of local availability. They take their holidays and traditions seriously, planning accordingly for proper revelry, feasting, and dancing. With feet as dexterous as their tongues, gnomes love to let loose, especially in the company of their compatriots. As with many humanoids, gnome cultures cherish regional variances; and with each of these differences come diverse cultures and palates.

Rock gnomes, typically identified by their oversize proboscises (thought to enhance their taste buds), are the most common and familiar of the gnomes. They approach life with an easy demeanor and a graceful adaptability, traits prevalent in their culinary customs as well. Unfussy by nature, they are just as comfortable dining on human stew or an elven fritto misto as they are on goat cheese–stuffed mushrooms.

Their brethren, the mysterious deep gnomes, are not. Svirfneblin, as they are known, are the most self-reliant and aloof of their kind, and often suffer an undeserved ill reputation because of their reclusiveness. Yet, these denizens of the Underdark are by no means evil or malicious, and they fuel their relentless pursuit of gemstones with a healthy yet simple diet of fresh fish, insects, and fungi.

The tinker gnomes, also known as Minoi, are almost exclusively found on the planet Krynn. Their devout commitment to invention is a manifestation of all gnomes' innate curiosity, but taken to the extreme. Experimentation, often without thesis, is a recipe for disaster as well as great progress. This has sparked inspired techniques in food preparation (baking and sous vide techniques) and preservation. Gnomes of the forest will walk a far simpler path, shunning the outside world (even fellow gnomes) and embracing all that nature has to offer. They are the shyest of the gnomes, and their self-imposed isolation has most certainly informed their eating habits. Proficient hunters and gatherers, forest gnomes are extremely sensitive to their ecosystem, thriving on roots and vegetables and preferring to prepare their food raw (meat excluded) and thoughtfully.

Gnomes feast and drink with aplomb, albeit with less variety than the others. Sweets and sugars are a rarity in the gnome diet, while spices and sauces are used sparingly, if at all. Traditional dairy products are usually not readily available, but some gnomes raise goats, which can yield butter, milk, and cheese. Yeast, both in bread and beverage making, is extremely uncommon. Gnomes do, however, excel at preparing meats and simple stews, as well as at foraging for fruits, vegetables, and various fungi.

TIEFLINGS: INFERNALLY BOLD

Like a runaway applecart in Waterdeep, tiefling dishes can take you by surprise and knock you over with their bold flavors. Sometimes referred to as a "race without a home," tieflings are a culture without a unified cuisine. Flavorings and spices take precedence over the proteins and produce that they season. Because all tieflings previously came from different groups prior to being cursed with the "blood of Asmodeus" and converted into their present devil-like states, their ingredients and dishes—which range from noodles, soups, and stews to vegetables, meats, and everything in between—are as varied as any throughout the planes. What changed when they were claimed by the Lord of the Nine

Hells, however, was a physiological shift of their palates and preferences. An area not known for its cuisine, the Nine Hells traditionally serves blackened, boiled, and bland foods, not meant to be enjoyed by its inhabitants. As terrestrial beings, tieflings typically rebel against these flavorings and crave the opposite: salty, sweet, tangy, and, most of all, spicy foods—robust flavors that cut through their charred taste buds and make them feel vigorous and alive.

Of course, some tieflings are more in tune with their infernal inclinations than others, which not only influences their conduct but also their food choices. For these tieflings, raw meat, marrow, blood, and sometimes even minerals and coal are the preferred menu, while mysterious magical concoctions smelling of sulfur, ash, and oil may quench their thirst. Regardless of their alignments, it would be a mistake to pre-judge these sometimes unfamiliar foods and eating habits. Tieflings know flavor, which can make them great chefs—provided you're willing to trust them enough to serve you.

HALF-ORCS: THE PALATE OF GRUUMSH

Half-orcs are the ultimate scavengers and foragers in the multiverse and the diversity in their diets proves it. Half-orcs are a traditionally nomadic people who have brought to the table flavors from both human and orc cultures. They are adroit omnivores who can find food in virtually any environment, but maintain a strong inclination toward meat, preferring it greatly to fruits and vegetables. That said, nuts and produce often make their way into their diets alongside various fungi, grubs, and insects. Practically nothing is off the table for a half-orc as long as the food meets two criteria: it fills you up and is worthy of a warrior.

In deference to their one-eyed warrior god Gruumsh, the true appetite of most half-orcs is adventure. However, half-orcs blessed with the proper time and resources will go to the trouble of cooking and seasoning their meats, salting their grubs, and even frying or drizzling chocolate upon those squirmy insects. Their non-picky palate and their generally jovial demeanor make them ideal dinner guests; but make sure to double, no triple, your order at the local butcher: at a muscular six to seven feet tall, half-orcs can *eat*, and eat big.

ARKHAN THE CRUEL'S FLAME-ROASTED HALFLING CHILI

Meat for the meat god! Understandably, the preparation of halfling is frowned upon in many realms, but their consumption is an important part of dragonborn cuisine. However, this recipe is rumored to be the personal one of Arkhan the Cruel, notorious disciple of the five-headed dragon goddess, Tiamat, and thus worthy of inclusion. You won't catch this ferocious and cunning Oathbreaker Paladin eating anything less than the finest halfling flesh in his chili, but the spices work wonderfully with any meat substitute you choose—in this instance, spicy ground turkey, or abyssal chicken, which is simmered for hours with kidney beans, allspice, cloves, cayenne, and a Vecna's handful of cocoa powder. This filling meat sauce can be consumed by the bowl or scooped on top of other beast (meat) or noodles.

In a small bowl, mix together the cocoa powder, chili powder, cinnamon, oregano, cumin, allspice, cloves, cayenne, ½ teaspoon salt, and ½ teaspoon pepper. Set aside.

In a blender or food processor, puree half the kidney beans with about ¾ cup of the broth until smooth and set aside.

In a small Dutch oven over medium heat, fry the bacon, turning it over as necessary, until well-rendered and lightly browned, about 13 minutes. Transfer the bacon to paper towels to drain, chop it, and reserve.

Return the pot to medium heat, add the onion and a pinch of salt to the rendered bacon fat, and cook, stirring occasionally, until softened, about 4 minutes. Add the garlic and the reserved spice mixture and cook, stirring constantly, until fragrant, about 1 minute more. Add the remaining 1¼ cups broth and bring to a simmer, stirring and scraping the bottom of the pot to loosen and dissolve any browned bits. Add the tomato puree, brown sugar, and pureed bean mixture and stir to incorporate. Add the ground turkey and break it into large chunks (it will break down more on its own). Add the remaining kidney beans and stir to mix. Adjust the heat to medium-high and bring to a simmer; then adjust the heat to medium-low and simmer to blend flavors and thicken slightly, stirring and scraping the bottom of the pot occasionally, about 30 minutes.

Add the vinegar and reserved bacon and stir. Taste and adjust the seasoning with additional salt and pepper, if necessary. Serve with oyster crackers or noodles, cheese, and onion, as desired.

SERVES 4 TO 6

1½ tablespoons unsweetened cocoa powder

1½ tablespoons chili powder

1¼ teaspoons ground cinnamon

1½ teaspoons dried oregano

¾ teaspoon ground cumin

½ teaspoon ground allspice

¼ teaspoon ground cloves

¼ teaspoon cayenne, or as needed

Kosher salt and freshly ground black pepper

2 (15-ounce) cans red kidney beans, drained and rinsed

2 cups low-sodium chicken broth

4 slices bacon

1 large yellow onion, finely chopped

5 garlic cloves, finely chopped

1 (15-ounce) can tomato puree

2 teaspoons dark or light brown sugar

1 pound lean ground turkey

1 teaspoon cider vinegar

Oyster crackers, freshly cooked buttered noodles, grated Cheddar cheese, and/or finely chopped onion for serving (optional)

COOK'S NOTE

The cocoa powder contributes both flavor complexity and a dark hue to the chili, without making it taste of chocolate. The cayenne gives a bare tingle, but you can certainly add more if you like your chili spicy-hot.

"Orc" Bacon

No, it isn't made from orcs—but *for* orcs. Half-orcs find this delectable snack quite to their taste, as do the goliaths of Eberron and a few game humans and halflings. It is said that a half-orc named Mazmorras was the first to discover this pungent recipe for cured pork strips, which you can practically taste from twenty yards away. Sometimes called "the Pork of Gruumsh," orcs flavor it with black pepper and garlic; a halfling might instead smooth off the edge with some maple syrup. Experienced adventuring parties venturing into orc lands know that dropping a bundle of bacon can throw pursuers off their trail, and orcs have even been known to barter with humans who carry it. For best results, try using Thayan Doomvault Swine Run pork—it has the right potency.

SERVES 4 AS A SNACK

1 pound thick-cut bacon

3 tablespoons light brown sugar

½ teaspoon freshly ground black pepper

1 teaspoon garlic powder

2 tablespoons orange juice

Preheat the oven to 375°F with a rack in the middle of the oven. Line a large rimmed baking sheet with foil. Coat a large wire rack with nonstick cooking spray and set it in the foil-lined pan.

Arrange the bacon slices on the rack, laying them tight against each other so the entire pound fits. Roast until they render some of their fat and shrink a bit, about 12 minutes.

Meanwhile, in a small bowl, mix together the brown sugar, pepper, garlic powder, and orange juice. Lightly brush the slices with about half of this brown sugar mixture and continue roasting until the brown sugar adheres to the bacon and the bacon appears glossy, about 7 minutes. Using tongs, turn over the slices. Lightly brush the slices with the remaining brown sugar mixture and continue roasting until the brown sugar mixture adheres to the bacon and the bacon appears glossy, 5 to 7 minutes more. Transfer the slices to a serving plate and serve warm.

FIRE-SPICED ABYSSAL CHICKEN KEBABS

There is no denying that a tiefling's distinct infernal heritage looms heavily over their identity. Some reject their unholy origins outright, but many proudly live in harmony with it, open to exploring all aspects of their unique traits. This open-minded approach has yielded a bold, unfettered diet that is often unapproachable and sometimes dangerous to the uninitiated. One dish they have a knack for is fire-spiced abyssal chicken (a bird-like fiend native to the Abyss and Avernus with a taste similar to fatty chicken), or fire-spiced anything for that matter since their natural resistance to heat has granted them an enhanced ability to handle spice as well. Flame-licked skewers of meat are dipped in a spicy, pepper glaze to create these kebabs with some serious kick.

If using wooden skewers, soak them in a bowl of water for 20 minutes prior to grilling.

In a bowl, whisk together the molasses, lime juice, and hot pepper sauce. Set aside.

In another bowl, whisk together the chili powder, brown sugar, paprika, onion powder, 2 teaspoons salt, and 2 teaspoons pepper to blend. Add the chicken and toss to coat.

Prepare a medium-hot fire in a charcoal grill or preheat a gas grill on high for 15 minutes.

Meanwhile, in a large bowl, gently toss the poblanos and onions (breaking up the onion chunks into pieces of two or three layers) with the olive oil, a pinch of salt, and a pinch of pepper. Stand two skewers side-by-side, ½ inch apart, with pointed sides facing up. Thread the set of double skewers with alternating pieces of chicken, onion, bacon, and poblano, making sure that the pieces are not too tight against each other; repeat with the remaining chicken, vegetables, and bacon. You should be able to make eight kabobs.

Grill the kebabs, turning every 3 minutes, until the onions and poblanos are tender and grill-marked, and the chicken is well-browned and cooked through, about 15 minutes. Brush the kebabs all over with the molasses mixture and grill for about 1 minute on each side (do not let them burn.) Remove the kebabs from the grill and let rest for about 3 minutes. Garnish with fresh mint and serve hot.

SERVES 4

3 tablespoons unsulphured molasses (not blackstrap)

1 tablespoon fresh lime juice

1 tablespoon hot pepper sauce

1½ tablespoons chili powder

2 teaspoons light or dark brown sugar

1 teaspoon smoked paprika

1 teaspoon onion powder

Kosher salt and freshly ground black pepper

2 pounds boneless, skinless chicken thighs (about 8), trimmed and cut into 1-inch pieces

3 large poblano peppers, seeded and cut into 1½-inch squares

2 red onions, halved lengthwise and cut into 8 equal chunks

1½ tablespoons extra-virgin olive oil

8 slices thick-cut bacon, each cut crosswise into 3 pieces

⅓ cup chopped fresh mint for garnish

COOK'S NOTE

Double-skewering helps prevent the pieces of food from spinning as you move the kebabs on the grill. Consequently, you will need sixteen skewers (wooden or metal) to make the eight kebabs.

HARDBUCKLER STEW

If you ever walk the streets of the walled gnome town of Hardbuckler, located just a few weeks east of Baldur's Gate by caravan, there's a good chance that you'll miss the real city altogether. While quaint country cottages connected by narrow footpaths crowd the surface, the true action is in their generous cellars, which can extend as many as three stories below the ground. Linked by tunnels that serve as underground thoroughfares, gnome residents run shoppes, inns, and taprooms out of these cozy, hearth-lit subterranean spaces. It's here you'll find the town's culinary specialty: Hardbuckler stew. Typically prepared with potatoes, mushrooms, lichens, turnips, and a miscellany of meats, from fowl and goats to shrews and voles, this earthy and aromatic stew hits all the right notes. While every establishment in this elaborate undercity will tell you that they prepare it "the right way," this particular version of the recipe calls for lamb, finely chopped for small gnome mouths.

SERVES 6

2 tablespoons neutral-tasting oil, such as vegetable, canola, safflower, or grapeseed

1½ pounds cremini mushrooms, quartered

Kosher salt

2½ pounds boneless lamb shoulder roast, trimmed of excess fat and cut into 1-inch chunks

Freshly ground black pepper

2 tablespoons all-purpose flour

1 large yellow onion, chopped

1 tablespoon finely chopped fresh thyme, or 1½ teaspoons dried

3 bay leaves

2 cups low-sodium chicken broth

1 pound turnip or rutabaga, peeled and cut into 1-inch pieces (about 4 cups)

1½ pounds Yukon gold potatoes, peeled and cut into 1-inch pieces

1 teaspoon sherry vinegar

½ cup chopped fresh parsley

In a large Dutch oven over medium-high heat, warm 1 tablespoon of the oil until shimmering. Add the mushrooms and ½ teaspoon salt and cook, stirring occasionally, until the mushrooms release their liquid and it evaporates, about 15 minutes. Adjust the heat to medium and continue cooking, stirring often, until the mushrooms brown, about 5 minutes more. Scrape the mushrooms into a bowl and set aside.

Meanwhile, preheat the oven to 325°F with a rack in the lower-middle of the oven.

In a bowl, toss the lamb with 1½ teaspoons salt, 1 teaspoon pepper, and the flour to coat. In the now-empty Dutch oven, warm the remaining 1 tablespoon oil over medium-high heat until shimmering. Add half the lamb so that the pieces are close together in a single layer but not touching (do not crowd pan) and cook, undisturbed, until deeply browned on the bottom, 3 to 4 minutes. Turn the pieces over and cook, undisturbed, until second side is deeply browned, 3 to 4 minutes more; transfer the lamb to a bowl. Repeat to brown the remaining lamb (adjusting the heat as necessary to avoid scorching); transfer to the bowl with the first batch.

Pour off all but 1 tablespoon fat from the pot. Return the pot to medium heat, add the onion, thyme, bay leaves, and 1 teaspoon salt and cook, stirring and scraping the bottom of the pot to loosen any browned bits, until softened, about 4 minutes. Add the broth, adjust the heat to medium-high, and scrape the bottom of the pot to loosen and dissolve any remaining

browned bits. Add the cooked lamb with its accumulated juices, stir to combine, cover, and bake for 40 minutes. Add the turnip pieces, submerge them in the liquid as best you can, replace the cover, and continue to bake for 30 minutes more. Add the potatoes and mushrooms, submerge them in the liquid as best you can, replace the cover, and continue to bake until the lamb and all the vegetables are very tender, about 1¼ hours more. If the stew is more liquidy than you'd like, mash some of the potatoes against the side of the pot to help thicken it.

Taste and adjust the seasoning with additional salt and pepper, if necessary. Remove the bay leaves, add the vinegar and most of the parsley, and stir to combine. Serve, sprinkling each serving with some of the remaining parsley.

TWICE-BAKED COCKATRICE WINGS

The tabaxi are long-tailed, feline humanoids known for their innately inquisitive and mercurial spirit, as well as agile hunting prowess. Also referred to as "Jaguar People" or "Leopard People" depending on their build and fur color, the tabaxi cat people of Maztica are particularly dangerous predators, but one still wonders how often they had the occasion to prey on cockatrices. Tabaxi are extremely particular about how they prepare their birds, and there is no denying that these extra-crispy chicken wings dusted with a zesty dry rub will please even the most finicky eater. The recipe is a jealously guarded secret and tabaxi can't keep their paws off them.

Preheat the oven to 300°F with a rack in the middle of the oven. Set a wire rack in a large rimmed baking sheet.

In a large bowl, toss the chicken wings with the baking powder to coat. Add the salt and pepper and toss again to coat. Arrange the wings skin-side up on the wire rack and roast for 40 minutes. Adjust the heat to 425°F and continue to roast until the wings are golden brown and crisp, about 40 minutes more. Sprinkle the wings with the garam masala and continue to roast for 10 minutes more. Using tongs, carefully remove the wings from the rack. Serve hot.

SERVES 4

3½ pounds chicken wings, halved at the joints, wing tips removed

1 tablespoon baking powder

1½ teaspoons salt

1½ teaspoons freshly ground black pepper

2½ tablespoons garam masala powder

COOK'S NOTE

The initial roasting at the lower oven temperature allows the fat to render, which aids in crisping the skin, as does the baking powder.

BRAISED LAMB

This rustic recipe for braised lamb is inspired by the culinary traditions of the Minmax half-orcs, a reclusive tribe that hails from the outskirts of Vaasa in the desolate Cold Lands of northeast Faerûn. They are known for extreme proficiency in combat, but mediocrity (or less) in just about everything else. Although several orc elders live among Minmax people serving as healers, shamans, and storytellers, the clan, led by the fearsome and wise Kalatuur Minmax, has embraced an atypical approach to food and politics. Similarly, their palate ranges greatly, from subtler human fare such as fish, cheese, and bread to the orcish desire for big-game meat. But this schism yields unexpected culinary benefits, including a profound approach to meat preparation that meshes distinct orcish flavors with human techniques. The Minmax clan prides itself on its battle prowess equally as much as this lamb braise, unparalleled in texture and flavor.

SERVES 4 TO 6

1½ tablespoons olive oil

15 garlic cloves, finely chopped

1½ tablespoons finely chopped fresh thyme

1 tablespoon finely chopped fresh rosemary

3½ pounds butterflied boneless leg of lamb, untied and netting discarded, if necessary

Kosher salt and freshly ground black pepper

2 teaspoons neutral-tasting oil, such as vegetable, canola, safflower, or grapeseed

½ cup dry vermouth

1½ pounds (about 5 cups) frozen pearl onions, thawed, drained, and blotted dry

2 teaspoons light brown sugar

3 tablespoons unsalted butter

1 teaspoon fresh lemon juice

¼ cup chopped fresh mint

In a small nonstick skillet over medium heat, mix the olive oil, garlic, thyme, and rosemary and cook, stirring, until it just begins to sizzle, 3 to 4 minutes. Scrape the mixture into a small bowl (you should have about ⅓ cup); remove 1½ tablespoons of the mixture and reserve separately.

With a sharp, thin-bladed (boning) knife, trim the fat, gristle, and silverskin from both the exterior and interior of the lamb. With the tip of the knife, make cuts in the larger muscles to help them flatten; cover the meat with plastic wrap and pound it to as even a thickness as possible. With the tip of the knife, lightly score the interior side of the meat with ¼-inch-deep cuts about 1 inch apart in a crosshatch pattern. Rub the greater quantity of the garlic-herb mixture over the scored surface, leaving a 1-inch border around the edges; sprinkle evenly with 1½ teaspoons salt and 1 teaspoon pepper. Roll the meat into a neat, compact cylinder, tucking in any loose bits and flaps as you go, and tie with kitchen twine at 1½-inch intervals, as well as once or twice lengthwise. Set the lamb aside at room temperature to rest for 1 hour.

Preheat the oven to 400°F with a rack in the middle of the oven. Dry the lamb with paper towels and generously sprinkle it all over with salt and pepper.

In a large ovenproof skillet over medium-high heat, warm the oil until shimmering. Add the lamb and brown well on all sides, turning it once every 3 minutes, for about 12 minutes. Transfer the skillet to the oven and roast until the center of the meat registers 120° to 125°F for medium-rare (or 130° to 135°F for medium to medium-well) on an instant-read thermometer, about 40 minutes.

Transfer the lamb to a carving board, cover loosely with foil, and let rest for about 15 minutes (the internal temperature will increase while the meat rests).

Meanwhile, taking care with the screaming-hot skillet, set it over medium-high heat. Add the vermouth and bring to a simmer, stirring and scraping the bottom of the skillet to loosen and dissolve any sticking bits. Add the pearl onions and ¾ teaspoon salt, return to a simmer, cover, and cook, stirring occasionally, for 5 minutes. Add the brown sugar and reserved garlic-herb mixture, stir to incorporate, and continue simmering, uncovered, until the onions are fully tender and the liquid in the pan is reduced to about 1 tablespoon, about 4 minutes more.

Remove the skillet from the heat, add the butter, and stir to melt and incorporate it. Add the lemon juice and pepper to taste and stir to incorporate. Taste and adjust the seasoning with additional salt, if necessary. Add most of the mint and stir to distribute.

Remove the twine, slice the lamb, and arrange on a warmed serving platter. Transfer the mint mixture to the platter with the lamb or into its own serving bowl, sprinkle with the remaining mint, and serve at once.

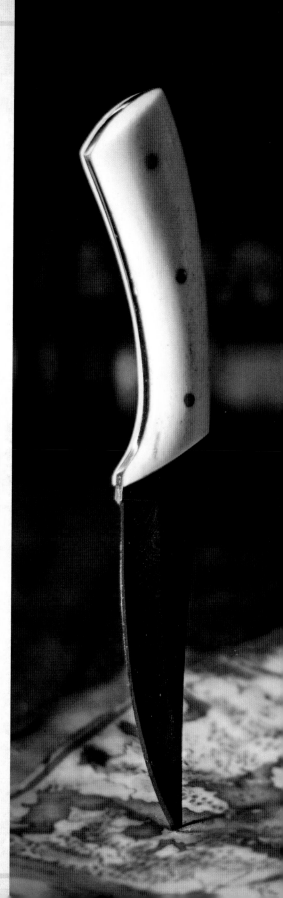

COOK'S NOTE

A boneless leg of lamb can take up to 30 minutes to trim. Because the leg includes muscles of varying thickness, use a sharp boning knife to cut slits in the meat and then pound the whole leg to even the thickness before rolling and tying it.

Deep Gnome Trillimac Pods

If it's the rare you're seeking, you've come to the right place. Trillimac fungus is among the most precious and temperamental plants of the Underdark, and only the deep gnomes of the City of Blingdenstone seem to know the secret of its cultivation and preparation. Traditionally prepared by cleaning, soaking, and drying the trillimac stalk, this subterranean staple makes a tasty sponge-like loaf that can last for weeks on the shelf—a popular item for trade or sale at the subterranean market of Mantol-Derith. What you won't find at the market, however, is trillimac pasta, which the distrustful svirfneblin keep only to themselves. Made with nutty trillimac stalk flour, this otherworldly pasta is filled with an earthy ragout made from the tops of this rare plant. One taste will have you foraging the Underdark for seconds. If you have trouble sourcing real trillimac pasta (and you will), thin wheat dough wrappers will do, but don't even think about substituting out the trillimac-top ragout.

In a large skillet over medium-high heat, warm 1 tablespoon of the olive oil until shimmering. Add the cremini mushrooms and ½ teaspoon salt and cook, stirring occasionally, until the mushroom liquid evaporates and they just start to sizzle and brown, about 12 minutes. Adjust the heat to medium, clear the center of the pan, add another 1 tablespoon olive oil, and allow it to heat for a moment. Add half of the onion and ¼ teaspoon salt and cook, stirring, until the onion softens, about 4 minutes more; stir the onion into the mushrooms. Add half of the garlic and cook, stirring, until fragrant, about 1 minute more. Add the sherry and cook, stirring and scraping the bottom of the pan to release and dissolve any browned bits, about 1 minute more. Scrape the ragout mixture into a bowl, add the parsley, and stir to incorporate. Set aside to cool to room temperature.

Wipe out the skillet, add the remaining 1 tablespoon olive oil, return the pan to medium heat, and warm until shimmering. Add the remaining onion and ½ teaspoon salt and cook, stirring, until softened, about 4 minutes. Add the remaining garlic and cook, stirring, until fragrant, about 1 minute more. Scrape the mixture into a medium bowl. Add the ricotta, egg, ½ cup of the Parmesan, ¼ teaspoon salt, and a few grinds of black pepper to the bowl. Stir until uniform, then set aside to cool to room temperature.

If you are using the dried mushrooms, in an electric spice grinder or mini food processor, pulverize the mushroom pieces until very, very fine and powdery. Add the powder to the ricotta mixture and stir until well blended.

CONTINUED ON PAGE 168 →

SERVES 6

3 tablespoons olive oil

1 pound cremini mushrooms, thinly sliced

Kosher salt

1 large yellow onion, finely chopped

7 garlic cloves, finely chopped

¼ cup dry sherry, such as Amontillado

3 tablespoons chopped fresh parsley

1¾ cups ricotta, preferably whole-milk ricotta

1 egg

1 cup freshly grated Parmesan cheese

Freshly ground black pepper

¼ cup small pieces dried mushrooms, such as porcini or shiitake (optional)

2½ ounces Italian Fontina cheese, shredded (about ¾ cup)

36 square wonton wrappers (from one 12-ounce package)

DEEP GNOME TRILLIMAC PODS, CONTINUED

In a small bowl, mix together the Fontina and remaining ½ cup Parmesan cheese.

Preheat the oven to 375°F with a rack in the middle of the oven. Coat a 12-cup muffin tin (preferably nonstick) with nonstick cooking spray.

To assemble, press one wonton wrapper into each cup, followed by about 1 tablespoon each of the ricotta mixture and mushroom ragout mixture, spreading each into an even layer. Add another wonton wrapper, rotating it slightly so the corners do not line up with the wrapper on the bottom. Repeat the layering with the remaining wonton wrappers and ricotta and mushroom ragout mixtures, always rotating the wonton wrappers, so the corners do not line up. Sprinkle about 1 tablespoon of the shredded cheese mixture evenly all the way to the edge of each cup; try to keep the cheese layer as thin as possible.

Bake until the cheese is melted, the edges of the wonton wrappers are browned, and the mini pies are hot all the way through, about 20 minutes, rotating the muffin tin 180 degrees halfway through the baking time.

Rest the mini pies for about 5 minutes. Use a dinner knife or small heatproof spatula to help remove them from the muffin cups (work carefully so they stay intact) and serve.

Surrogate Steaks

The multiverse is a stranger place than many dare imagine. In a bizarre ruin near the Barrier Peaks of Oerth, otherworldly humanoids had stocked their pantries with all manner of sustenance sealed within clear airtight pouches. When the sole survivor of an expedition to that cursed place returned to Greyhawk, she claimed to have made the journey home eating the curious meat she found there. After much puzzling by local alchemists over the remaining stock she carried, they determined it was not a meat at all but a curious vegetable compound seasoned to deliver the essence of meat. Inspired by this discovery, some bold chefs began experimenting with their own approaches to this "surrogate steak," a process eventually perfected by high elves relying on soy, barley, and cocoa butter.

SERVES 4

1½ pounds plant-based ground meat, such as Impossible Burger

1 tablespoon soy sauce

2 teaspoons garlic powder

1 tablespoon finely chopped fresh thyme

Kosher salt

2½ tablespoons freshly and very coarsely ground black pepper

1 tablespoon neutral-tasting oil, such as vegetable, canola, safflower, or grapeseed

1 shallot, finely chopped

2 garlic cloves, finely chopped

½ cup brandy or cognac, plus 1 tablespoon

1 cup low-sodium vegetable broth

⅓ cup heavy cream

½ teaspoon light brown sugar

2 teaspoons grainy mustard (optional)

½ teaspoon fresh lemon juice

1½ tablespoons snipped fresh chives

Preheat the oven to 200°F with a rack in the middle of the oven.

In a large bowl, break up the meat into coarse chunks. Add the soy sauce, garlic powder, 1½ teaspoons of the thyme, and ¾ teaspoon salt. Mix to distribute the seasonings fully, but do not overmix. Shape the mixture into two "steaks," about 5 inches in diameter and 1¼ inches thick.

Spread the pepper in a wide, shallow dish, such as a pie plate. Dredge one side of each steak in the pepper, pressing lightly to make it adhere.

In a large nonstick skillet over medium-high heat, warm 1½ teaspoons of the oil until shimmering. Add the steaks, unpeppered-side down, and cook undisturbed until well-browned on the bottom, about 4 minutes; if the skillet becomes too smoky at any point, adjust the heat accordingly. Adjust the heat to medium, turn the steaks peppered-side down, and cook undisturbed for 2 minutes more. Transfer the steaks to an ovenproof plate, tent loosely with foil, and place it in the oven to stay warm. Pour off any fat accumulated in the skillet and wipe it out.

Add the remaining 1½ teaspoons oil to the skillet over medium heat, and warm until shimmering. Add the shallot, remaining 1½ teaspoons thyme, and ½ teaspoon salt. Cook, stirring, until the shallot is barely softened, 1 to 2 minutes. Add the garlic and cook, until fragrant, about 1 minute more. Add the ½ cup brandy and cook until reduced slightly, about 1 minute more. Add the broth, adjust the heat to medium-high, and bring to a simmer. Continue cooking, stirring occasionally, until the liquid is reduced by almost half, about 5 minutes. Add the cream and sugar and cook, stirring, until the liquid is reduced slightly and coats the back of a spoon, about 2 minutes. Remove from the heat; add the mustard (if using), 1 tablespoon brandy, lemon juice, and 1 tablespoon of the chives; and stir to incorporate. Taste and adjust with salt, if necessary. Spoon the sauce over and around the steaks and sprinkle with the remaining chives. Serve at once.

Barovian Butterscotch Pudding

After a delectable wolf steak, some buttery garlic bread, and a few glasses of Red Dragon Crush wine, nothing satisfies the sweet tooth like the Blue Water Inn's famous Barovian butterscotch pudding. This dish is as sweet and smooth as a tall chalice of owlbear milk. But a few pieces of advice for those who seek to traverse the ghostly mists of Barovia to dine in their establishments: (1) return home before nightfall, especially during the full moon; (2) don't spend the night at Castle Ravenloft, no matter how much the host wants you to stay; and (3) avoid dream pies and Purple Grapemash No. 3 by the Wizard of Wines vineyard at all costs!

In a heavy saucepan over medium heat, combine the butter, brown sugar, water, corn syrup, lemon juice, and salt. Bring to a boil, stirring occasionally to melt the butter and dissolve the sugar. Continue cooking at a rolling boil, stirring occasionally, until the mixture registers 240°F on an instant-read or candy thermometer, about 3 minutes. Adjust the heat to medium-low and simmer gently (the mixture should bubble lazily and steadily—if not, adjust the heat accordingly), stirring frequently, until the mixture registers 300° to 310°F on the thermometer and has a bittersweet, borderline burnt fragrance, about 6 minutes more.

Meanwhile, in a bowl, whisk together the cream and milk to combine. In another bowl, whisk the yolks, cornstarch, and a little of the cream-milk mixture until uniform; take care to work out any tiny lumps of cornstarch.

Remove the pan with the brown-sugar caramel mixture from the heat. Very carefully pour in about ½ cup of the cream-milk mixture; the mixture will bubble, steam, and possibly splatter. Whisk vigorously, but with care, for about 1 minute, reaching into the corners of the pan. If some of the caramel mixture is seized or still stuck in the corners of the pan, it will re-melt and loosen again. Return the pan to medium heat and, whisking constantly, add the remaining cream-milk mixture; continue whisking until any bits of seized caramel have melted fully and the mixture just reaches a simmer, about 3 minutes.

CONTINUED ON PAGE 172 →

SERVES 4

¼ cup unsalted butter

⅔ cup packed dark brown sugar

2 tablespoons water

1½ tablespoons light corn syrup

1 teaspoon fresh lemon juice

¾ teaspoon kosher salt

¾ cup heavy cream

2 cups whole milk

3 egg yolks

3 tablespoons cornstarch

1 teaspoon pure vanilla extract

1 tablespoon Scotch or Irish whiskey (see Cook's Note)

Very lightly sweetened whipped cream for serving

Barovian Butterscotch Pudding,
CONTINUED

◆— COOK'S NOTE —◆

Avoid using a heavily peated Scotch, which can overwhelm the dish with smokiness.

Whisking constantly, gradually add about ½ cup of the caramel to the egg yolks. Again whisking constantly, add the egg mixture to the pan and continue to cook, whisking constantly, for 1 minute more. Remove from the heat, add the vanilla and Scotch, and whisk to incorporate.

Set a fine-mesh strainer over a bowl. Pour in the pudding and, with a flexible spatula, fold and stir the pudding gently to work it through the strainer. With a piece of parchment paper or plastic wrap, cover the pudding, pressing the paper or wrap directly onto the pudding surface.

Refrigerate until cold and set, at least 4 or up to 24 hours. At serving time, stir the pudding gently until smooth, then top with the whipped cream.

FRIED FINGERS

A dish popularized by the lizardfolk of Saltmarsh, where it was commonly prepared with humanoid parts instead of poultry, these succulent, breaded strips give a new meaning to the term "finger food." Today, this recipe is served throughout all civilized parts of the multiverse, featuring pulled strips of locally sourced fowl, rolled in an unconventional seasoned breading, baked crisp, and served with dwarven mustard, tiefling tomato-molasses, or a warm plum dipping sauce. If you do have occasion to try the original, fatty halfling fingers work best.

SERVES 4

PLUM SAUCE

1 tablespoon neutral-tasting oil, such as vegetable, canola, safflower, or grapeseed

¼ cup finely chopped scallion whites

Kosher salt

2 teaspoons finely grated fresh ginger

1 large garlic clove, finely chopped

¼ teaspoon five-spice powder

1 cup plum jam or preserves

1½ tablespoons plain rice vinegar

1 tablespoon soy sauce

1 tablespoon light brown sugar

Freshly ground black pepper

MAKE THE SAUCE. In a small saucepan over medium heat, warm the oil until shimmering. Add the scallion whites and a pinch of salt and cook, stirring, until softened, 1 to 2 minutes. Add the ginger, garlic, and five-spice powder and cook, stirring, until fragrant, about 1 minute. Add the jam, vinegar, soy sauce, brown sugar, and pepper to taste and whisk to combine. Bring the mixture to a simmer, stirring, 3 to 5 minutes. Adjust the heat to low and continue simmering and stirring to blend the flavors, about 1 minute. Scrape the sauce into a microwave-safe container and set aside.

Preheat the oven to 325°F with a rack in the upper-middle of the oven. Line a large rimmed baking sheet with foil.

MAKE THE CHICKEN FINGERS. Spread the panko in an even layer on the foil-lined baking sheet and bake until golden brown, 8 to 10 minutes, stirring several times. Scrape the toasted panko into a wide, shallow dish, add the crushed potato chips, mustard powder, garlic powder, cayenne, 1¼ teaspoons salt, and a few grinds of pepper. Stir to distribute the potato chips and seasonings. In a second wide, shallow dish, spread the flour. In a third wide shallow dish, whisk the eggs, a pinch of salt, and a few grinds of pepper until well blended.

Adjust the oven temperature to 500°F and fit a wire rack into the foil-lined baking sheet.

Blot dry the chicken strips and sprinkle lightly with salt and pepper. Working with several pieces of chicken at a time, dredge them in the flour and tap off any excess. Dip the floured chicken pieces into the egg mixture to coat thoroughly, allow any excess egg to drip off. Then dredge them in the panko mixture to coat thoroughly, pressing it onto the chicken to help it adhere. Carefully transfer the chicken pieces to the rack on the baking sheet (they should not overlap) and coat them with cooking spray.

Bake until the coating is deep golden brown and crisp and the chicken fingers are cooked through (they will feel firm when squeezed gently with your fingertips), 10 to 12 minutes, checking them frequently, turning them over and coating the second side midway through the cooking time and rotating the pan 180 degrees for even cooking. Cool the chicken fingers for about 4 minutes.

If the sauce has cooled completely and you want to serve it warm, cover the dish, and microwave briefly to reheat. Taste and adjust the seasoning with additional salt and pepper, if necessary. Serve the fried fingers hot, passing the sauce on the side.

CHICKEN FINGERS

2 cups panko bread crumbs

3 cups packed kettle-cooked potato chips (about 5 ounces), crushed to fine crumbs

2 teaspoons dry mustard powder

2 teaspoons garlic powder

Pinch of cayenne, or to taste

Kosher salt and freshly ground black pepper

½ cup all-purpose flour

2 eggs

4 boneless, skinless chicken breasts (6 to 8 ounces each), cut on the lengthwise diagonal into ¾-inch-wide strips

Olive oil cooking spray

COOK'S NOTE

A good method for crushing the potato chips is to put them in a resealable bag and roll over it repeatedly with a rolling pin until the chips are finely crushed.

BYTOPIAN SHEPHERD'S BREAD

Perhaps no cuisine among the planes could be more otherworldly than that of the aasimar, the far-flung descendants of celestials. But even aasimar are half-human, and their need for mortal sustenance is why many believe the bread recipe common in the Twin Paradises is ultimately aasimar in origin. This spiced bread, served in thick slices, is made from grains imbued with grated carrots and rich chunks of almond. It makes a delicious day-starter for the hardy shepherds who work the pastoral valleys of Bytopia. Bold adventurers, take note: If you ever find yourself in possession of the rare herb known as shiftspice, sprinkle a liberal pinch into the batter to ensure that each loaf yields a totally unexpected flavor.

MAKES ONE 8½-INCH LOAF

2 cups all-purpose flour

2 teaspoons baking powder

½ teaspoon baking soda

2 teaspoons ground ginger

1 teaspoon ground cinnamon

½ teaspoon freshly ground nutmeg

1 teaspoon kosher salt

½ cup currants

3 eggs

¾ cup packed light brown sugar

¼ cup unsalted butter, melted and cooled

⅓ cup buttermilk

1 teaspoon pure vanilla extract

1 pound carrots, peeled and coarsely grated (about 3 cups)

½ cup slivered or sliced almonds

Preheat the oven to 350°F with a rack in the middle of the oven. Lightly oil or butter a 8½ by 4½-inch nonstick loaf pan.

In a bowl, whisk together the flour, baking powder, baking soda, ginger, cinnamon, nutmeg, and salt to combine. Add the currants and stir to distribute.

In a large bowl, whisk together the eggs and brown sugar until well blended. Add the melted butter and whisk to combine thoroughly. Add the buttermilk and vanilla extract and whisk to combine thoroughly. Stir in the carrots. Add the dry mixture and, using a flexible spatula, fold and stir until the wet and dry ingredients are just incorporated; do not overmix. Scrape the batter into the prepared pan and smooth the top. Sprinkle the almonds evenly over the batter and press them very lightly to help them adhere.

Bake until the almonds on top are golden, the edges of the loaf pull away from the pan, and a toothpick inserted into the center comes out clean, about 55 minutes, rotating the pan 180 degrees midway through the baking time.

Cool the pan on a wire rack for about 15 minutes. Turn the loaf out, place it right-side up onto the rack, cool to room temperature, and serve.

6

ELIXIRS & ALES

"'I know you've got something in one of your pouches that would take the chill off the dwarf's bones, if you know what I mean,' Tanis said softly.

'Oh, sure, Tanis,' Tas said, brightening. He fumbled around, first in one pouch, then another, and finally came up with a gleaming silver flask. 'Brandy. Otik's finest.'"

—MARGARET WEIS AND TRACY HICKMAN, *DRAGONS OF AUTUMN TWILIGHT*

E ven with all of the extraordinary variety in the multiverse, every culture, plane, and world seems to have one thing in common: everyone drinks! And there is no shortage of beverages to accompany the recipes in this book. Drinks move between cultures more freely than foodstuffs, so it is hard to pin a given concoction to its origin. Elves may be given to wine, and dwarves to ale, but gather some adventurers in a bar, and most will prove just as daring in their tastes as they are in their heroic exploits.

Some even say that you can't fully appreciate food without a fine drink pairing. Whether you need an uplifting cup of tea, a thirst-quenching juice infusion, or something a bit harder to take the edge off, the taverns of the multiverse await your patronage. Cosmopolitan bartenders have elevated the invention of drinks to an art that rivals alchemy for its complexity and cleverness—their creations can seem downright magical; and sometimes, they are.

Unfortunately, there is only space here for a few noteworthy libations. To get a thorough knowledge of drinks in the multiverse would require an epic quest to the edges of reality itself because in every corner of the known worlds, no matter what the materials at hand, someone has figured out a way to get tipsy. There are potions, palate cleansers, beer, ciders, spirits, ales, wines, juices, enhanced waters, natural springs, coffees, teas, and cozy glasses of warm bedtime milk to be had out there.

The recipes collected here have all blazed a path through the realms to become mainstays of the adventuring lifestyle. The most popular concoctions have their own regional names and variations, catering to the sense of humor and the taste buds of the locals, so it never hurts to know a few nicknames for your favorite potent potable.

Cheers!

PAR-SALIAN'S TEA

Whether you're a warrior doffing your plate mail after an arduous adventure or a wizard relaxing after a studious session in the stacks, each day demands time for repose. From an obscure oolong to a common chamomile, teas are imbued with incredible calming and restorative effects for the body and soul. The powerful white-robed Highmage Par-Salian was renowned for his arcane prowess, but those close to him warmly recounted his potent tea leaf homebrew as well. A single saucer full of this extraordinary blend, which was known to include a fresh ginger infusion with honey, chamomile, dried lemon, orange peel, and a dash of slippery elm bark (granting it a smooth, oily aftertaste) among its components, was said to soothe even the most dogged cold—an effect that ensured the survival of one of Par-Salian's most famous students, Raistlin Majere. Numerous interpretations of Par-Salian's legendary tea remain popular throughout Krynn, with some iterations steeped with rare and psychedelic bekial seeds from the thorn bushes of Estwilde, though it is said that none, save for his most trusted students, could successfully replicate his herbal amalgam.

Using a vegetable peeler and working vertically, remove the zest from the lemon in wide strips (it should produce eight strips). Slice the ginger into four pieces, each about ½ inch thick, and working with one slice at a time, use the bottom of a sturdy mug or the flat side of a chef's knife to smash them. Place two lemon zest strips and one piece of smashed ginger in each of four mugs. Add about 1¼ cups boiling water to each mug and steep until fragrant, about 4 minutes. Add honey to taste to each mug and stir to combine. Holding the mint sprigs by their stems, slap them against the back of your hand or forearm (to help release their fragrance). Add one sprig to each mug and serve.

SERVES 4

1 lemon

2½-inch piece fresh ginger, peeled if desired

5 cups boiling water

Honey as needed

4 sprigs fresh mint

COOK'S NOTES

Peeling the ginger isn't strictly necessary.

The ginger and lemon zest will continue to infuse the liquid as you drink. For the strongest flavor, leave them in the mug until you finish; remove them at any point when you find the flavor sufficiently potent.

> *"Par-Salian opened his mouth to speak, then realized Highmage Astathan was studying him very intently. He closed his mouth again. The tea lingered with a slightly oily aftertaste on his tongue, and Par-Salian finally recognized it. It was bekial seed from the thorn bushes of Estwilde; it acted to open one's consciousness without the deleterious effects of most other opiates. A little was enough to put its user in a trance. Too much was toxic. And the fine line between the two was only drawn by master herbologists."*
>
> **—LUCIEN SOULBAN,** *RENEGADE WIZARDS*

Mushroom Tea

When the hearth fire dims in the Underdark, the drow are known to reach for their kettles—not to make any herbal tea, but instead an after-dinner broth of simmering mushrooms. If they can find them, the drow prefer matsutake, though shiitake or maitake will do in a pinch. They place the sliced mushrooms into a clear broth seasoned with dried kelp, sometimes with a splash of fish stock or soy sauce and alcohol, and heat it in a teakettle. From this, they pour small cups of the fragrant tea to imbibe slowly until the mushrooms cook to perfection, at which point they are eaten with a fine skewer.

SERVES 4

2 (5- to 6-inch long by 3-inch wide) strips kombu (dried kelp), lightly wiped with a damp cloth

4½ cups water

2 ounces (about 5) fresh shiitake mushrooms, stems removed and caps very thinly sliced

1 tablespoon soy sauce

¾ teaspoon kosher salt, or to taste

2 tablespoons sake

2 scallions, white and light green parts, thinly sliced, for garnish

In a saucepan, submerge the kombu in the water and let rest until softened, about 30 minutes. Set the pan over medium heat and bring the water to a simmer, 10 to 12 minutes. Remove the kombu and discard. Adjust the heat to medium-high and bring the liquid to a boil, about 3 minutes. Stir in the shiitakes, soy sauce, and salt. Cook, stirring occasionally, until the shiitakes are tender, 1 to 2 minutes. Stir in the sake. Taste and adjust the seasoning with additional salt, if necessary. Serve, sprinkling a portion of the scallions over each serving.

COOK'S NOTES

Sometimes packages of kombu are labeled "Dashi Kombu" (dashi being the traditional Japanese broth of which kombu is a main component).

Serve this savory tea in mugs, for sipping, along with spoons for eating the mushrooms and scallions.

EVERMEAD

Crafted from a secret Evermeet recipe and aged for hundreds of years, a sip of this splendid elven concoction is "a taste of the higher planes themselves." Superlatives aside, in the culinary realm, it is undeniably the beverage by which all others are measured. Smooth and aromatic, this extraordinary elixir blankets the palate with powerful notes of clover honey and a mélange of elven fruits and grains that are so rare they don't even have a name in the common language. Rumored to use ingredients and techniques similar to feywine, this pricey draught is only available on the Isle of Evermeet in the Trackless Sea west of Faerûn or in *Aurora's Catalogue* by hand keg or bottle. If you ever are lucky enough to try the original, make sure to drink slowly—it can just as quickly intoxicate as inspire. This recipe, though, is crafted sans alcohol to preserve your better judgment.

In a saucepan over medium heat, warm the cinnamon sticks and cloves until fragrant, about 2 minutes. Carefully add the water (it may sputter) and ginger, adjust the heat to medium-high, and bring the mixture to a simmer. Add the honey, jam, and a tiny pinch of salt and return to a simmer, whisking to dissolve the honey and jam. Adjust the heat to low, partially cover the pot, and simmer to blend the flavors, about 20 minutes. Cover the pot completely, remove it from the heat, and let steep for 20 minutes more. Strain the mixture into a bowl or other container. Serve warm, at room temperature, or lightly chilled.

SERVES 4

2 cinnamon sticks, broken in half

8 whole cloves

4 cups water

1-inch piece fresh ginger, peeled, cut into 3 or 4 slices, and smashed

¼ cup honey

6 tablespoons seedless blackberry or boysenberry jam

Kosher salt

COOK'S NOTE

If you prefer the alcoholic version of Evermead, add about 1½ ounces of vodka or brandy per serving, garnish with a twist of orange.

DWARVEN MULLED WINE

Pronounced by dwarven diplomats "the finest mulled wine this side of the material plane," this mixed beverage is a multicultural affair. Originally crafted to celebrate the signing of the Swordsheath Scroll, which ended the Kinslayer War and sealed a treaty between the Thorbardin dwarves and the nearby Qualinesti elves of Krynn, dwarven drinksmiths combined their own full-bodied dragon's wine and local spices with delicate, fresh fruits provided by the Qualinesti. The result was a perfectly balanced, spicy and sweet concoction that satisfied and warmed the insides of both groups as they spent cold winters constructing their shared fortress of Pax Tharkas. Years later, during the War of the Lance, this recipe was popularized by Lord Gunthar, Grand Master of the Knights of Solamnia, who would serve it to visiting knights (and himself) as a favorite nightcap. Flavored with orange slices, brown sugar, cinnamon, and cloves, this fruity and full-bodied wine packs a dwarven-size punch, but is sure to thaw your bones during Yuletide or any other time of year.

SERVES 4

2 juice oranges, such as Valencia

8 whole cloves

⅓ cup packed light brown sugar, or to taste

1 (750-ml) bottle medium-bodied, fruity red wine, such as Merlot or Syrah

1 cinnamon stick

⅛ teaspoon pure vanilla extract

3 tablespoons brandy, or to taste

COOK'S NOTES

The flavor of mulled wine improves with rest, so consider starting it several hours ahead of time. Reheat it gently, careful to avoid boiling (which can cause an oxidized taste), then remove the aromatics and add the vanilla and brandy.

Mulled wine recipes vary widely. This one is heavy on the orange, light on the spice and sweetener, and includes brandy for a modest potency boost. However, it can be customized with different liqueurs such as Grand Marnier, Cointreau, or St-Germain, and spices such as cardamom pods, black peppercorns, or whole allspice.

Using a vegetable peeler, remove the zest from the oranges in wide strips; reserve one strip for each drink and refrigerate, covered, until serving time. Stick the cloves into two or three of the remaining zest strips and set aside. Cut the zested oranges in half and juice them (which should yield about ¾ cup juice).

In a large saucepan over medium heat, bring the orange juice and brown sugar to a simmer, stirring to dissolve the sugar. Add the wine, cinnamon stick, and orange zest (including the clove-studded pieces) and bring to a simmer. Adjust the heat to medium-low and simmer, partially covered and stirring occasionally, until the wine is fragrant and infused, about 1 hour (do not allow it to boil). Add the vanilla and brandy and continue to simmer, stirring occasionally, to blend the flavors, about 2 minutes more. Taste and adjust the flavor with additional brown sugar and/or brandy, if necessary. With a slotted spoon, remove and discard the cinnamon stick, orange zest, and cloves.

Meanwhile, fill one small mug or heatproof glass for each drinker with hot water to preheat them, about 2 minutes. Empty the mugs or glasses, ladle some of the wine into each, garnish with one of the reserved orange zest strips, and serve at once.

COCOA BROTH

A warm hearth, a cozy chair, and a steaming mug of chocolatey, liquid goodness—for a halfling this is the Seven Heavens (the Green Hills of Venya to be exact). Rumored to be the result when a halfling mage cast *wish* to find the perfect fireside beverage, this salty, sweet, and spicy cocoa creation tickles every part of the palate and cheers every part of the soul. Infused with coffee and spices from a far-off region of Toril called Tukan, just add some marshmallow to this beverage, pick up a good book or scroll, and you can call it a night.

SERVES 4

½ cup unsweetened cocoa powder, preferably Dutch-processed

½ cup packed light brown sugar, or to taste

¾ teaspoon ground cinnamon

½ teaspoon ground cardamom

Pinch of kosher salt

1 cup water

2½ cups whole milk

1 teaspoon pure vanilla extract

1½ cups espresso or very strong black coffee, hot

In a saucepan over medium heat, whisk together the cocoa powder, brown sugar, cinnamon, cardamom, salt, and water until smooth. Bring the mixture to a simmer and cook, whisking constantly, for about 2 minutes, making sure the whisk gets into the edges of the pan. Whisk in the milk and bring to a simmer (do not boil), whisking frequently, about 10 minutes. Whisk in the vanilla and espresso. Taste and adjust the flavor with additional brown sugar, if desired. Divide among four mugs and serve.

Hot Spiced Cider

Hot spiced cider is an essential seasonal drink with appeal to all seeking warm liquid refuge after a day on the trail. Fresh-pressed apple cider, usually sold by the jugful at marketplaces or farms, is simmered over a low fire or stove with allspice, cloves, brown sugar, and a burst of orange tossed in for measure before it's topped with fresh cream and a cinnamon stick. Halflings serve up their own special varietal named Moonslake, a minty, alcoholic apple cocktail that's been blended with a boiled and strained mint-crushed water yielding a biting, cool aftertaste (that humans tend not to enjoy). Elves prepare it clean, often cheesecloth strained, for a refined, glassy amber appearance. Dwarves aren't fussy, they just like it spiked. Regardless of your preference, savor one of these cool-weather concoctions to warm you from the inside out.

Using a vegetable peeler, remove the zest from the orange in wide strips; reserve one strip for each drink and refrigerate, covered, until serving time. Stick the cloves into two or three of the remaining zest strips and set aside. (Reserve the orange for another use.)

In a large saucepan over medium heat, warm the allspice and cinnamon sticks, stirring, until fragrant, 1 to 2 minutes. Remove from the heat and carefully add the cider (it will sputter vigorously), cranberry juice, brown sugar, and the clove-studded orange zest strips. Adjust the heat to medium-high and bring to a simmer, stirring to dissolve the brown sugar. Adjust the heat to medium-low and simmer, partially covered and stirring occasionally, to infuse the cider mixture, about 20 minutes. Cover the pot completely, remove from the heat, and let steep for 20 minutes more.

Set a fine-mesh strainer over a large heatproof bowl. Pour in the cider, discard the solids, and return the mixture to the saucepan. Over medium heat, return the cider to a simmer. Add the vanilla, stir, taste, and adjust the seasoning with additional brown sugar, if necessary.

Meanwhile, fill one small mug or heatproof glass for each drinker with hot water to preheat them, about 2 minutes. Empty the mugs or glasses, ladle some of the cider into each, garnish with one of the reserved orange zest strips and a couple of cranberries (if using), and serve at once.

SERVES 4

1 large orange

8 whole cloves

1 teaspoon whole allspice berries, coarsely crushed

2 cinnamon sticks

3 cups apple cider or unfiltered apple juice

2 cups pure cranberry juice

3 tablespoons light brown sugar, or as needed

Pinch of kosher salt

¼ teaspoon pure vanilla extract

Fresh cranberries for garnish (optional)

GOODBERRY BLEND

Few spells in a druid or ranger's repertoire are as handy or nutritious as a well-timed casting of Goodberry. A single "goodberry," transmuted by drawing upon the divine essence of nature itself, can provide an adventurer with a full day of nourishment; some have denoted their enchanted healing properties. But despite any druidic lore or magic, one thing is certain: this healthy blend of field berries boosted by green essentials, banana slices, honey, and a pinch of salt will provide anyone with the vital essentials needed to start the day's journey.

Put the ice in a blender and pulse to crush. Add the orange juice, spinach, honey, and salt; pulse to begin breaking up the greens. Blend to liquefy the solids, 20 to 60 seconds, depending on your blender. Add the blueberries and banana and blend until the mixture is uniform, thick, and moves easily in the blender jar, about 45 seconds. Pour into four cups and serve immediately.

SERVES 4

½ cup ice cubes

1½ cups orange juice

1 cup packed baby spinach

3 tablespoons honey

Pinch of kosher salt

2 cups frozen blueberries, partially thawed

1 sliced banana, frozen

COOK'S NOTE

For a more robust flavor, consider adding 1–2 tablespoons of fresh ginger to the blend.

Delayed Blast Fireball

It's no coincidence that the mixed drink known as the Delayed Blast Fireball received its moniker from the famed damage-dealing wizard incantation. Sometimes referred to as "firestar wine," this sweet and syrupy concoction with a cinnamon inflection is layered with flavors and packs a serious punch that does justice to its arcane namesake. The spiced bourbon and spicy pepper flakes form a lethally delicious combination that goes down easy but delivers its full effects several rounds of beverages into the night.

MAKES ABOUT 1¾ CUPS

1½ cups bourbon

½ teaspoon crushed red pepper flakes, or more to taste

5 cinnamon sticks, broken in half

¼ cup packed light brown sugar

⅓ cup hot water

In a clean glass jar with a lid, combine the bourbon, red pepper flakes, and cinnamon sticks. Screw on the lid, shake, and store in a cool, dark place to infuse for 5 days, shaking the jar at least once a day.

In a bowl, whisk the brown sugar and hot water to dissolve the sugar fully and set aside to cool to room temperature, about 10 minutes. Line a fine-mesh strainer with cheesecloth, set it over the bowl with the brown sugar mixture, and strain the bourbon into it.

Wash and dry the jar and return the firestar wine to it. Serve or store in a cool, dark place for up to 3 months.

COOK'S NOTES

The ½ teaspoon of crushed red pepper will provide a noticeable, moderate heat. If you prefer a more intense heat, use up to 1 teaspoon. You can give the drink more flavor nuance by replacing the crushed red pepper flakes with toasted chile. Toast half of a small dried California, pasilla, or guajillo chile in a dry skillet over medium heat until fragrant, 4 to 5 minutes. Cool the chile and tear into very small (½-inch) pieces. For extra heat, use some of the chile seeds as well.

This drink can be enjoyed neat, over ice, mixed with cola, or as the foundation of an excellent hot toddy with spiced chai.

THE MINDFLAYER

Vodka stored at subzero temperatures is combined with fresh ginger and grape juice (for a hazy purple hue) and finely crushed ice. It is served so cold that if your first frosty gulp doesn't zap you with a mind-numbing brain freeze, then the alcohol blast that hits right after just may! Variations of this popular chilled beverage (sometimes referred to as "Cone of Cold" or "Shondath Icewine") are aplenty across the Sword Coast.

In a blender, combine the ginger, sugar, and lime juice until the solids are a very, very fine puree and the mixture is uniformly syrupy, about 1 minute. Set a fine-mesh strainer over a measuring cup or bowl and strain the mixture, stirring and pressing on the solids to extract as much syrup as possible (you should have about ½ cup). Discard the solids and return the syrup to the blender.

Add the grape juice concentrate, vodka, and ice and blend until the ice is finely crushed and the mixture is uniform and moves easily in the blender jar (the timing will depend on the power of your blender). Divide the mixture between two roomy highball or Collins glasses, garnish with the grapes (if using), and serve at once, with straws if desired.

SERVES 2

3 tablespoons peeled and chopped fresh ginger

¼ cup sugar

⅓ cup fresh lime juice

½ cup thawed grape juice concentrate

5 ounces vodka, cold

3 cups small ice cubes or coarsely crushed ice

Several black or red seedless grapes for garnish (optional)

ROLLRUM

The picturesque city-state of Tashalar is known for its jeweled coasts, temperate climes, and abundant vineyards, as well as for one of its most famed exports—rollrum. This dusky, licorice-infused tonic is noted for bright, herbal tones and a minty finish. Establishments of the highest pedigree, ranging from the Elfsong Tavern in Baldur's Gate to the Lady Luck in Daggerford (as well as a slew of questionable taprooms), offer up homebrewed incarnations of this absinthe-style classic. For those not inclined to partake in alcoholic imbibement, but who are still seeking a minty beverage, try elven sprucebark quaff, which also serves as a potent palate cleanser.

SERVES 2

1½ tablespoons sugar

1½ ounces water

20 large mint leaves, plus 2 sprigs for garnish

Small ice cubes or coarsely crushed ice

4 ounces absinthe

4 ounces seltzer, cold (optional)

In a cocktail shaker, muddle the sugar and water until the sugar dissolves and the liquid is syrupy. Add the mint leaves and muddle gently to bruise them and release their fragrance (do not pulverize). Fill the shaker about halfway with ice and add the absinthe. Cover and shake to blend and chill, 30 seconds. Fill two chilled old-fashioned, rocks, or small Collins glasses about halfway with ice and divide the mixture between them. If using, add half the seltzer to each and stir gently to blend. Holding the mint sprigs by their stems, slap them against the back of your hand or forearm (to help release their fragrance), garnish each glass with a sprig, and serve at once.

COOK'S NOTES

Although less potent in terms of alcohol content, you can substitute other anise-flavored liqueurs, such as pastis, Pernod, Herbsaint, or even ouzo, for the absinthe.

POTION OF RESTORATION

Every adventurer needs a pick-me-up now and again, and nothing slakes the thirst and dulls an ache quite like a Potion of Restoration. Fruity and sweet, with tones of blackberry and lemon, the gin hides away until you already feel its fire in your belly. Barkeeps imbue it with a pinch of butterfly pea, which gives it a distinctive blue color—in a dimly lit dungeon, you might even mistake it for its magical namesake. But then again, if you drink enough of these, you will know neither pain nor fear . . . though you may not be undertaking any glorious feats either.

SERVES 2

15 large blackberries

1 tablespoon sugar

1½ ounces fresh lemon juice

3 ounces gin

½ teaspoon butterfly pea powder (optional)

Roughly cracked or small ice cubes

1 ounce crème de mure (blackberry liqueur)

2 lemon zest twists for garnish

In a cocktail shaker, muddle together 11 of the blackberries, the sugar, and lemon juice until the sugar dissolves fully. Add the gin and butterfly pea powder (if using). Fill the shaker about halfway with ice. Cover and shake to blend and chill, 30 seconds. Fill two chilled old-fashion or rocks glasses about halfway with ice and strain half the mixture into each, then pour ½ ounce crème de mure over the ice in each. Run one lemon twist around the rim of each glass and drop it in; add two of the remaining blackberries to each glass and serve at once.

═══════════ ● COOK'S NOTES ● ═══════════

The drinks have a purple hue from the muddled blackberries, but to make the color extra vibrant, use the butterfly pea powder, which creates a vivid magenta color in the presence of an acid, such as lemon juice. Butterfly pea powder is available online and at some natural foods stores with a good selection of herbs and spices.

Crème de mure is a blackberry liqueur. If you can't find it, crème de cassis, a black currant liqueur, is a fine substitute.

Zzar

There isn't a human-run tavern on the Sword Coast that doesn't serve some form of Zzar, a northwest Faerûnian bar staple. Often pricier than lager or stout, this nut-flavored, orange-hued refreshment is often crafted by fortifying sluth (a sparkling white wine) with an almond liqueur. Some barkeeps substitute amaretto for a liqueur that mimics the taste of almond but forgoes nuts entirely in favor of herbs and spice, while others add their own twists to the tried-and-true recipe. In any case, the desired result is a smooth and creamy nut drink with a strong kick and a vibrant aftertaste that might include subtle variations ranging from sweet or tangy to salted or roasted.

Using an electric handheld mixer, a whisk, or a stand mixer fitted with the whisk attachment, beat the cream and sugar together until thickened and the whisk just begins to leave a trail. Add ½ ounce of the amaretto and beat briefly, until the cream is very softly whipped; refrigerate until needed.

Fill a cocktail shaker about halfway with ice and add the remaining 3 ounces amaretto, the coffee liqueur, and milk. Cover and shake to blend and chill, 30 seconds. Place two ice cubes in each of two chilled old-fashioned or rocks glasses and divide the mixture between them. Very gently spoon a portion of the whipped cream into each glass so it floats on the surface of the liquid and serve at once.

SERVES 2

¼ cup heavy cream, cold

1 teaspoon confectioners' or granulated sugar

3½ ounces amaretto

Small ice cubes

1½ ounces coffee-flavored liqueur, such as Kahlua

½ cup whole milk

COOK'S NOTE

The ice in the shaker provides sufficient dilution, especially since there are no hard spirits in the cocktail, which is why the quantity of ice in the glasses is limited.

CHULTAN ZOMBIE

Located on the southwestern coast of Faerûn stands Port Nyanzaru, the last bastion of civilization before an untamable expanse of undead-infested jungles, perilous rivers, and oversize alpha predators. You may have seen a massive Tyrannosaurus rex in the flesh, but you haven't really been to Chult unless you've tried the "zombie," a rustic, fruit juice cocktail composed of indigenous produce, local liqueurs, and a medley of rums. Served in massive wooden bowls at nearly every eatery in town, the Chultan Zombie boasts an enticing velvety, saccharine flavor that hides the waves of alcohol lurking beneath the surface. Wild fresh flavors collide on your taste buds making it feel as if Elminster cast a charm spell *in* your mouth. A word to wise travelers: Refrain from chugging a bowl of this before you go dinosaur hunting . . . or do, if you need the added boost of liquid inspiration. A version of the "zombie" showcasing a medley of local fruits is served at watering holes on the precipice of the jungle frontier of Q'barra on Khorvaire. Other variations include a just-as-delectable non-alcoholic variety from the Flanaess, perfect for young adventurers.

Fill a cocktail shaker about halfway with ice and add the rum, pineapple juice, orange juice, grenadine, lime juice, Cointreau, and bitters. Cover and shake to blend and chill, 30 seconds. Fill two chilled Collins or highball glasses about halfway with ice. Strain half the mixture into each. If using, add 1½ ounces seltzer to each glass and stir gently. Garnish each cocktail as desired and serve at once.

COOK'S NOTES

If you don't have any Cointreau to add sweetness and flavor, you can substitute 1½ teaspoons superfine sugar to each drink. To make superfine sugar, simply spin regular granulated sugar in the blender or food processor to break down the crystal size, which will allow it to dissolve in liquid more readily.

This is a high-volume drink, and cocktail shakers vary in size; so you may have to prepare the cocktails one at a time. Boston shakers, the type used in most bars, are larger than cobbler shakers with built-in strainers, which are common for home use.

SERVES 2

Roughly cracked or small ice cubes

5 ounces amber or dark rum

4 ounces fresh pineapple juice

2 ounces fresh orange juice

1½ ounces grenadine

1 ounce fresh lime juice

½ ounce Cointreau or Grand Marnier

4 dashes Angostura bitters

3 ounces seltzer, cold (optional)

2 orange slices, pineapple chunks, and/or maraschino cherries for garnish

AFTERWORD: PLAYING WITH YOUR FOOD

Playing Dungeons & Dragons is nothing if not a social experience. You get together with your adventuring companions, and you laugh, you sweat, you cry, and you bond. And you probably eat. That is after all the meaning of the word "companion," the people you break bread with.

The recipes in this book are designed for D&D fans who want to grow their bond with their companions by sharing delicious dishes grounded in the D&D multiverse. While these recipes stand on their own merits, it's only natural that they might also serve to reward a hungry party who has just saved the day—or to energize one who is about to.

To help make your experience with this cookbook fit in with your gaming, here are a few ground rules and suggestions for making your adventure culinary.

Rule #1: *Support*. If you are the Dungeon Master (DM), it might be best to leave the cooking to someone else. You are already doing all of the preparatory work for the adventure. Many DMs offer up their homes for play, and if you are hosting, you may feel responsible for keeping everyone else fed. So, players, show your thanks to the DM by volunteering to bring the food!

If your group plays at your friendly local game store, or some other public space that likely does not have a full kitchen, you should think ahead. You might find a fridge and a microwave there that can hold a few Tupperware containers, if you are lucky. Some dishes that you can prepare ahead of time that will transport well to a game include the Underdark Lotus with Fire Lichen Spread or Halfling Oatmeal Sweet Nibbles. If you know you have

an oven for heating up food when you get there, then you might consider bringing Sword Coast Seafood Bouillabaisse or Chicken-Something Dumplings.

Don't forget that cooking and eating can both make a mess, but not all dishes are equally messy. Some recipes that don't require players to have their own plates and utensils include Iron Rations, Hand Pies, Bytopian Shepherd's Bread, and Fried Fingers. But wherever you are bringing the food, figure out how to deal with any leftovers, and how to avoid leaving a dish disaster in your wake.

One fun way to use this cookbook is to try to match the food your group eats with the adventure you are playing. Experiencing the cuisine of a particular region of the Forgotten Realms, for example, can help players and DMs alike get immersed in the setting.

Rule #2: *Plan*. Plan serious meals for the beginning or end of a play session. If you are doing a real marathon, and you need to have a full meal in the middle, then take a break from the game. Some of the dishes in this cookbook, like Quith-pa and Delzoun "Tide-Me-Overs," make for good snacks around the table, but if you're laying out a multicourse cornucopia, you're going to need the table space. As a rule of thumb, if you need to have utensils and plates to eat, then set the dice and character sheets aside until you're done. You don't want to have to fish a d4 out of your Community Cheeses.

After all, there's nothing better than taking an hour after a D&D session to decompress with your friends over a refreshing dinner, chatting about the ups and downs of the adventure. These post-game sessions can actually make a big difference in your campaigns—it helps everyone to get on the same page about game events, and it may even lead to some inspirations for the next session. And if your session runs all night, there are some great breakfast options in this book, like the Stuffed Egg-Battered Toast.

There are a few ways to integrate eating into the play of D&D. If you know in advance that the party is going to attend a banquet, you can always arrange to have the meal ready for the players to enjoy in real-time as they roleplay their characters. This requires some coordination, but it can really bring the game world to life, along with a little mood lighting, music, and maybe even costumes.

But if you're going to build a meal into your D&D session, you probably aren't going to be able to make it from scratch during a quick break. Choose dishes where most of the preparatory work can be done before the session starts, where it will only take a few minutes to heat things up and get them on the table. Traveler's Stew and Potato Leek Soup are examples of good choices where you can do a lot of the work beforehand and then heat them up at the last minute. You definitely want to avoid trying to make something such as Pan-Fried Knucklehead Trout while you are in the middle of a play session, because if you get distracted and leave it cooking for too long (like a knucklehead), it could easily get ruined and the smell of this rare aquatic treat will no doubt linger until next week's session.

Rule #3: *Improvise*. Every DM knows that sometimes you just have to wing it—that rules are guidelines, and that to keep up the flow of play you may have to do what seems right rather than leafing through rulebooks. Every chef knows the same rule: you have to work with what you've got, and sometimes that means taking a path different than the printed recipe. Most important, these recipes are intended to inspire your creativity. Once you have a sense for the palate of each of the cultures and regions, you can use that as a building block for developing your own recipes in the spirit of these guidelines. If your group takes a liking to recipes such as Elven Marruth, why not try making a variation that captures the spirit of elven cuisine by fusing it with a bit of pulled pork or bacon?

Once you get the hang of it, you can develop your own recipes. And if you are having trouble deciding between ingredients, remember that you are a D&D player—you can always roll for it! For example, you could assign tofu, chicken, pork, and beef each to a number on a d4. Give it a roll, and whatever number lands becomes the accompanying protein for those tasty Kara-Tur Noodles. But like any good DM, if the result of the die roll doesn't feel right, don't be afraid to exercise a little "divine intervention" and reroll. Sometimes it takes a die roll to tell you what your real preference would be.

Dine on!

ACKNOWLEDGMENTS

As dedicated Dungeons & Dragons players and Dungeon Masters, we grew up poring over a wide variety of D&D products, all of which taught us a new vocabulary of the imaginary through its art and gameplay. Only now as directors and writers, can we begin to understand the far-reaching effects the game and its art had on our burgeoning imaginations, informing our ability to conceptualize and tell stories. Accordingly, we want to first thank everyone who contributed to creating and expanding upon this incredible game over the last forty-five years. We continue to draw inspiration from the game and feed these ideas back to the world in the media we create, forming a cycle of creativity that all leads back to this amazing game.

In order to bring a project with this broad a scope and this much complexity to market, it certainly took a village. This book wouldn't have been possible without the help, support, and dedication of dozens of individuals beyond the author team. For starters, much love and thanks to our families and friends—while too many to count, they are our constant source of love, support, and inspiration. Next, to the people and organizations that truly made this piece possible: thank you to the incredible efforts and talents of publisher Aaron Wehner (who conjured the book idea with the D&D team), Emma Rudolph (editor), Kelly Booth (creative director), Emma Campion (deputy creative director), Kimmy Tejasindhu (production editor), Shaida Boroumand (approvals coordinator), Dan Myers (production manager), Mari Gill (production designer), Ray Katchatorian (photographer), Valerie Aikman-Smith (food stylist), Glenn Jenkins (prop stylist), Conceptopolis (illustrators), Tamara White (photo retoucher), Jane Chinn (color manager), Hannah Rahill (SVP backlist strategy and development), Daniel Wikey (assistant marketing director), Windy Dorresteyn (VP of marketing), Lauren Kretzschmar (publicity manager) and the rest of the team at Ten Speed Press, who shared our passion and vision for this project. Our sincerest thanks and appreciation to the team at Wizards of the Coast, D&D's publisher and our licensing partner, who not only allowed this project to take place but helped us with amazing insights. Special thanks to Nathan Stewart, Liz Schuh, Hilary Ross, Adam Lee, Christopher Perkins, Mike Mearls, Jeremy Crawford, Greg Tito, David Gershman, Shauna Narciso, and all the other fine folks who helped us. This is not to forget the incredible recipe developer and chef responsible for making a delicious reality of the fantasy dishes we compiled and conceptualized—our infinite thanks to Adam Ried! Also, a warm thank-you to Matthew Lillard of Beadle and Grimm, Joe Manganiello of Death Saves, and Stefan Pokorny and Nate Taylor of Dwarven Forge, who all loaned us many amazing artifacts from their respective companies and collections, as well as Justin Goby Fields of Sanctum Studios, who custom-made several of our D&D magical items. A hearty thank-you to our literary agent, Jacques de Spoelberch, who flawlessly managed the business side of things and offered us continuous support and guidance. Last, but not least, a very special thank-you to all of the D&D designers and artists over the years who truly made this book possible.

ABOUT THE AUTHORS

KYLE NEWMAN is a Hugo Award-nominated author and award-winning filmmaker who has directed numerous feature films including the *Star Wars*-fueled comedy *Fanboys* starring Kristen Bell and Seth Rogen and the action-comedy *Barely Lethal* starring Samuel L. Jackson and Hailee Steinfeld for A24 Films. He has created music videos for the industry's top artists including Lana Del Rey ("Summertime Sadness") and Taylor Swift ("Style"). Kyle also produced the critically acclaimed documentary *Raiders!: The Story of the Greatest Fan Film Ever Made*, as well as the thriller *Happily* alongside Jack Black. He also crafted the story for the Netflix Original animated feature *Gnome Alone*. In 2018, Penguin Random House published his first book *Dungeons & Dragons: Art & Arcana*—a history of the world's preeminent role-playing game—to great acclaim including nominations for Locus and Hugo Awards. Newman, an honors graduate of NYU's Tisch School of Film/TV and a member of the Directors Guild of America, resides in Los Angeles with his two sons.

JON PETERSON is widely recognized as an authority on the history of games. He co-authored *Dungeons & Dragons: Art & Arcana* (2018), which was a finalist for a Hugo Award. His book *Playing at the World: A History of Simulating Wars, People and Fantastic Adventures, from Chess to Role-Playing Games* (Unreason Press, 2012) revolutionized games scholarship with its rigorous source-driven methodology. Frank Lantz, director of NYU's Game Labs, called *Playing at the World* "the best book that's ever been written about one game." The *Village Voice* called it "the first serious history of the development of Dungeons & Dragons." The book is frequently taught at a university level, and Jon often lectures on games history at universities, conferences, and conventions. He has contributed to academic anthologies on games, including MIT Press's *Zones of Control* (2016) and Routledge's *Role-Playing Game Studies: Transmedia Foundations* (2018). Jon also writes for various games and geek culture websites, including Boing Boing, the Escapist, and Gamasutra, as well as maintaining his own blog.

MICHAEL WITWER is a bestselling author known for his work on the Hugo-nominated *Dungeons & Dragons: Art & Arcana* (2018) and the critically acclaimed *Empire of Imagination: Gary Gygax and the Birth of Dungeons & Dragons* (Bloomsbury, 2015). He holds degrees from Northwestern University and the University of Chicago and has a diverse professional background that has ranged from his current position as communications director of a national healthcare services firm to significant work in the gaming market. Through his work as an author, Michael has been featured on NPR's *All Things Considered*; spoken at Google, Pixar, and Lucasfilm; and served as a featured speaker at many of the top gaming conventions and book festivals. His books have won many honors, including being selected as an Amazon "Best Book of the Month," a GeekDad "Best Book of the Year," a Geek.com pick for "Best Coffee Table Books," and the *Irish Examiner*'s 2018 "Best Book," while his other writings have appeared on Slate.com, Tor.com, Signature-reads.com, and GeekDad, where he is a regular contributor. Michael resides in Chicago, Illinois, with his wife, two daughters, and two sons.

INDEX

Text, cover illustration, and interior illustrations copyright © 2020 by Wizards of the Coast LLC. Dungeons & Dragons, its logo, D&D, and the dragon ampersand are trademarks of Wizards of the Coast LLC in the USA and other countries.
All Rights Reserved.
Photographs copyright © 2020 by Ray Katchatorian.
Some illustrations incorporated into page art copyright © Shutterstock.

All rights reserved.
Published in the United States by Ten Speed Press,
an imprint of Random House,
a division of Penguin Random House LLC, New York.
www.tenspeed.com

Ten Speed Press and the Ten Speed Press colophon are registered trademarks of Penguin Random House LLC.

Library of Congress Cataloging-in-Publication Data
Names: Newman, Kyle, 1976- author. | Peterson, Jon, author. | Witwer, Michael, author.
Title: Heroes' feast : the official Dungeons & Dragons cookbook / by Kyle Newman, Jon Peterson and Michael Witwer.
Description: First edition. | New York : Ten Speed Press, 2020.
Identifiers: LCCN 2020022809 (print) | LCCN 2020022810 (ebook) | ISBN 9781984858900 (hardcover) | ISBN 9781984858917 (ebook)
Subjects: LCSH: Cooking. | Nutrition. | LCGFT: Cookbooks.
Classification: LCC TX714 .N529 2020 (print) | LCC TX714 (ebook) | DDC 641.5—dc23
LC record available at https://lccn.loc.gov/2020022809
LC ebook record available at https://lccn.loc.gov/2020022810

Hardcover ISBN: 978-1-9848-5890-0
eBook ISBN: 978-1-9848-5891-7
B&N Special Edition ISBN: 978-1-9848-5936-5

Printed in Canada

Illustration on cover and pages xxviii, 50, 82, 112, 146, 172 by Conceptopolis LLG

Publisher: Aaron Wehner
Editor: Emma Rudolph
Production editor: Kimmy Tejasindhu
Art director and designer: Kelly Booth
Photo director: Emma Campion
Production designer: Mari Gill
Production manager: Dan Myers
Color manager: Jane Chinn
Photo assistants: Dane Christensen, Tyler Demogenes
Food stylist: Valerie Aikman-Smith
Food stylist assistant: Morgan Baker
Prop stylist: Glenn Jenkins
Prop stylist assistant: Zachary Wine
Photo retoucher: Tamara White
Recipe developer: Adam Ried
Approvals coordinator: Shaida Boroumand
Copyeditors: Andrea Chesman, Patrick Barb
Proofreader: Linda Bouchard
Indexer: Ken DellaPenta
Publicist: Daniel Wikey
Marketer: Lauren Kretzschmar

Wizards of the Coast Team: David Gershman, Shauna Narciso, Adam Lee, Hilary Ross, Liz Schuh

10 9 8 7 6 5 4 3 2 1

First Edition